FREEDOM

From Bondages

FREEDOM
From Bondages

Marilyn Hickey

Marilyn Hickey Ministries
P.O. Box 10606
Denver, Colorado 80210

ISBN 0-914307-29-0

CONTENTS

Chapter 1
Freedom From Bondages . . . . Page 7

Chapter 2
Freedom From Fear . . . . Page 23

Chapter 3
Freedom In Tests and Trials . . . . Page 45

Chapter 4
Freedom From Poverty . . . . Page 65

Chapter 5
Freedom From Insecurity . . . . Page 85

Chapter 6
Freedom From Sorrows . . . . Page 105

Chapter 7
Freedom From Wrong Eating Habits . . . . Page 129

Chapter 8
Freedom From Fiasco . . . . Page 149

Chapter 9
Freedom From Depression . . . . Page 169

Chapter 10
Freedom In A Right Self Image . . . . Page 189

Chapter 1

FREEDOM FROM BONDAGES

What is a yoke, and how is it representative of Christian service? Find out how the yoke of Christ will free you from any yoke of bondage in your life, and how it will cause you to maintain perfect balance in your Christian walk.

Very frequently I find that believers have difficulty in accepting the Christian service to which Christ has called them. They aren't sure about which direction He is leading them, contrary to the Scripture in which Jesus Himself confessed, *"My sheep know my voice, and the voice of a stranger they do not follow."*

Why do not more sheep hear the voice of Christ calling them into a faith that grows and abounds with the fruit of the spirit? It is because while they have accepted the resurrection of Christ for salvation, they have neglected the yoke of His service. Instead, they are weighted down by a yoke of bondage.

In Matthew 11:30 Jesus told us to take His yoke upon ourselves. Just as a yoke joins two oxen together to make them more easily directed by the farmer, the yoke of Christ joins His Body together to be led in one direction by Him.

But the Bible speaks of another type of yoke, and it is one Christ wants to free us from: that is, the yoke of bondage. The word "yoke" has three meanings: 1) to link yourself with something in order to work; 2) to couple two things together; and 3) to denote balance (I thought this was interesting).

What are you yoked to? If you are yoked to Jesus Christ then your Christian walk will be marked by temperance, or **balance.** But the yoke of sin is one of ups and downs, snaring your faith to throw you out of balance. Your goal in the freedom of the Spirit-filled life ought to be one where all your attitudes and actions are consistent with God's Word. Any other yoke will distract you from your call, becoming a bondage and a hard task master.

THE YOKE OF SIN

"The yoke of my transgression is bound by His hand: they are wreathed, and come up upon my neck: he hath made my strength to fall, the Lord hath delivered me into their hands, from whom I am not able to rise up" (Lamentations 1:14).

Here Jeremiah is saying, "I sowed sin, and now it has trapped me. I am unable to bring myself out of it."

He's right, for only God can free us from sin's bondage. Sin is a robber that steals God's strength from your life. Its weight upon the soul is so great that Jeremiah said, *"The yoke of bondage has come upon my neck."* Why his neck? Because when bondage to sin enters your life, you find yourself bowed down to it, for it is impossible to serve two masters.

Sin always operates in that manner. At first you start with a seemingly innocent choice and you say, "Just once won't hurt anything."

For instance, in smoking cigarettes someone will tell you, "I can quit any time."

As soon as you hear yourself excusing something this way, watch out. Be aware of statements that are basically saying, "I can sin today, and not tomorrow." With cigarettes, soon the person is smoking two, three, and they're back to the old habit which had them bound before.

I hear people make the same excuses for their drug habits, believe it or not. They'll say, "One little puff of marijuana doesn't have any hold over me, I can take it or leave it."

But when you choose sin it isn't long before instead of

you controlling it, it is controlling you. It is a very subtle trap which begins with "choices," but ends in bondage. You end up hating it, but you are bowed down to that sin just the same. Sin is a very real yoke of bondage.

THE YOKE OF THE LAW

This yoke is an entirely different type of bondage; in fact it looks just the opposite. Yet although it may appear different, its weight is just as heavy!

"Now therefore why tempt ye God, to put a yoke upon the neck of the disciples, which neither our fathers nor we were able to bear?" (Acts 15:10).

Most Christians will say, "I don't smoke, I don't drink, I don't swear. I don't even go to movies!"

But soon they imagine that all of their "don'ts" are what is making them worthy to receive God's grace, rather than remembering that they received God's grace in spite of their works—not because of them! They have slipped into the bondage of the law, and this is the yoke which was destroying the Jewish faith in God.

Self righteousness relies on the fact that you don't sin intentionally, so in essence you end up thinking, "I am right with God because I haven't sinned."

You are right with God because of His grace toward you. The yoke of the law is Satan's trick to make Christians start acting as "God's appointed judges," and that is a dangerous trap!

I am not condoning sin. I would never say, "Oh, it's all right for you to commit adultery—just as long as it's in moderation."

If that were the case, why not go ahead and steal or murder in moderation? Sin is sin, and God hates it. But on the other hand, He hasn't called us to minister condemnation to others. If you have been putting other believers down instead of building them up, you need to be delivered from the yoke of the law.

Most Christians who have yoked themself to the law have another characteristic: they condemn themselves as much as they condemn others. They'll say, "If I don't read twenty chapters of the Bible, God will be upset with me!"

I encourage you to read as much of God's Word as possible; but when you start trying to "earn your way to heaven," then you are yoked to the Law. We could never earn any of God's goodness and mercy; He just loves us so much that He gives mercy and grace anyway!

The consciousness of the law is evident in the story of the prodigal son. After the young man left home he squandered his whole inheritance on his wild, sinful lifestyle. He must have been wild if he could spend all of that money in such a short time! Then after the money was gone, his "friends" were also gone. He ended up in a pigsty, trying to share their food and they were getting more to eat than he was. He reasoned, "My father's slaves eat more than I. I'm too terrible a person to be his son, so maybe he'll let me be a slave."

What was that? The yoke of legalism that says: "I'm not good enough for this; so maybe if I **work** I can get favor."

The son poorly misjudged his father, because when he arrived home, the first thing his father did was come running, throw his arms around him, and welcome him warmly. He said, "You are still my son, and I love you. You won't be my slave, you'll always be my son."

He welcomed his loved one home by celebrating the occasion with a tremendous feast, greater than any they had ever had.

How our human minds and legalistic attitudes try to squelch the abundance of God's mercy toward us. We forget that He says, "You're My child," whether we deserve it or not—and none of us deserve it, do we?

The yoke of the law will give you a negative, poor self image where you say, "I could never meet God's standards," and you feel so unworthy. Oh, you are always trying to meet them, but your efforts are directed by the flesh, rather than on the ability of His spirit.

The yoke of the law puts faith at a standstill because you no longer try to please God by faith; you fail to see yourself as worthy to be His child. But while you and I aren't worthy in ourselves, His worthiness far outweighs our shortcomings. Look to Jesus' ability, not your own, and you won't be bowed down by the yoke of the law.

Don't get caught up in trying to "work your way" into the Father's grace, trying to earn His kindness. Those actions are motivated by insecurity and not realizing what He's already done for you. Then, because you feel so negatively about yourself, you start seeing others in the same light: "Well...I know he repented, but he'll have to prove himself to me."

Or you say, "He may be a Christian, but he doesn't do many spiritual deeds. He's wrong; I'm right."

Let me say that I often notice more people winning souls to the Lord through the "wrong" technique than those who are so busily pointing the finger. Take heed to the advice of Acts 15: the yoke of the law was too heavy for the Jewish forefathers to bear during their day; it is too dangerous for you to assume now.

THE UNEQUAL YOKE

Paul illustrated why Christians and unbelievers should not be yoked together, and the imagery is strong:

> *"Be ye not unequally yoked together with unbelievers: for what fellowship hath righteousness with unrighteousness? and what communion hath light with darkness? And what concord hath Christ with Belial? or what part hath he that believeth with an infidel? And what agreement hath the temple of God with idols?"* (2 Corinthians 6:14-16a).

You won't find any common ground between lovers and haters of God. The proof is found in the Greek word for "fellowship," which is **koinonia.** Its meaning is "to have in common."

The definition for a believer, a "new creature in Christ," is actually "a being which never before lived." You were made alive, and Paul asks, "What do life and death have in common?" The obvious answer is "nothing."

Yet I know that many Chistians choose to spend more time around unbelievers than with their believers. They will prefer an unbeliever who is totally skeptical and unhearing toward the Gospel, and they'll claim, "My life is a witness. She's my best friend, so what else matters?"

Here is what matters: more often than not the unbeliever's life will influence the Christian to turn back. Soon she finds that she has conformed to the world's standards, rather than being transformed by the renewing of her mind. Plainly, you probably won't get your mind renewed if the majority of your time is spent in fellowship with an unbeliever.

Believers who knowingly yoke themselves to unbelievers in marriage find that their lives present even more difficulty. They marry in spite of what the Scripture warns, not realizing how tiring the unequal yoke becomes.

I thought, "Marriage shows the idea of two partners walking together in the same direction down life's road."

With an unequal yoke you have two partners, each one pulling in his or her own direction. Where is the balance? There is none, and my heart breaks as I watch Christians being worn down to compromise by the pressure of an unequal yoke.

If you are married to an unbeliever, take heart. God has promised that the believing mate will sanctify the household. Hold on to your faith and don't give up. Your diligence in faith and prayer is going to pay off.

You say, "I don't have any worldly friends. My mate is a Christian. So how does this concern me?"

The Bible also warns not to keep close fellowship with Christians who intentionally live in sin. Sin is contagious, and God doesn't want you "catching it." I want to encourage you to seek out friends whose level of faith you admire. Choose friends whose lives are godly examples, whose maturity gives you a goal to aspire toward. Sin may be contagious, but faith is even more contagious, and you can catch that, too. Just take advantage of every opportunity to commune with stronger, more mature Christians than yourself.

I believe the Body of Christ should be full of a contagious faith. People can come into our local churches and catch faith from us. They won't catch condemnation or pity—there is enough of that in the world! That's what they want to get free from. Instead, they will catch faith and holiness because we are a church which is free from yokes of bondage.

If you want to influence others in such a way, then be free from bondage and yoke yourself to Jesus Christ. If there is an idea of bondage in your life, then you have already taken your first step towards overcoming it. Perhaps you have had a habit, or maybe it was a negative attitude. Whatever the sin, your first decision involves repenting from it and turning away from it. Jesus wants to free you because He said, *"I came to set at liberty those who were bruised."*

The yoke of bondage is a bruise on your soul; but Jesus doesn't point his finger at your bruised areas and say, "Naughty, naughty." Instead He says, "I want to heal those bruises. I want to set you free from the destruction of bondage." And He has several ways of giving you freedom:

MIRACLES

Did you know that God has miracles specifically for breaking yokes of bondage? Some people have bondages that appear impossible to break. We look at them, shake our heads, and wonder why they can't get with it. Then they'll attend one certain service, and before five minutes have passed, a tremendous release takes place as the miracle-working power of God hits them. They are instantly set free:

"I am the Lord your God, which brought you forth out of the land of Egypt, that ye should not be their bondmen; and I have broken the bands of your yoke, and made you go upright" (Leviticus 26:13).

God says, "I don't want you being a bondslave of sin. I want to free you from that spiritual Egypt and bring you into the promised land."

Once a woman who attended our church in Denver was bound by a horrible emotional and mental oppression that even had her looking for help in a local psychiatric hospital. After she came out, her husband would bring her to services and she would sit there in a fog, looking as though she was 1,000 miles away because she was so heavily sedated. Then one night as the teaching came forth from the pulpit, it was as if a steel band around her head was instantly torn loose. Immediately she saw everything in crystal clear perspective, for God had set her free with His miracle power. Just as He broke the bondage of oppression for that woman, He'll do it for you.

FASTING

I have known many people with deep personality problems who were literally transformed through fasting. It is an excellent way to be set free from a yoke of bondage:

"Is not this the fast that I have chosen? to loose the bands of wickedness, to undo the heavy burdens, and to let the oppressed go free, and that ye break every yoke" (Isaiah 58:6).

I am a firm believer in the practice of regular fasting.

Every Christian should lead a fasted life, not just fast as a once-a-year or one-shot thing. Some Christians fast whenever they hit a trouble spot, but when I see that I wonder, "If you were already fasting and prepared, would you even be experiencing this trouble?"

People who fast consistently are consistently victorious. A lot of people are their own worst enemies, and they know it. Their bondage is not some outward sin or habit; rather, it is a poor personality. They will tell me, "I can't help but be negative. Someone is always mad at me; I always say the wrong thing."

The personality is one area where the saying truly applies, "A leopard cannot change his spots." But God can change a leopard's spots, can't He? Fasting can transform the most difficult areas of your life because it allows God to deal with the areas you can't control.

My question is, "Are you willing to deny your flesh in order to gain spiritual victory?"

I strongly recommend that you set a portion of your week to fast. If you only fast two meals each week (and go aside for prayer during those times), you will see yokes of bondage destroyed and you will move into the victory of freedom.

Finally, examine your heart to make sure you really desire freedom from bondage. Do you want it enough to do something about it? Many Christians lack freedom for the saddest reason of all: because they don't want to be free.

JESUS' NAME

Jesus already won your freedom for you, and Galatians 5:1 tells you how to bring His freedom into your life:

"Stand fast therefore in the liberty wherewith Christ hath made us free, and be not entangled again with the yoke of bondage" (Galatians 5:1).

The authority of Christ's name is what will keep you free from yokes of bondage, once you have been set free. Philippians 2:9 tells us that Jesus' name is above every name. Is His name above temptation to sin? Is His name above bondages? Certainly it is. Jesus purchased your freedom with His blood, and then He gave you the authority of His name to continue in His liberty. The responsibility has become yours to stand fast in it.

Instead of letting the enemy drag you back into an area of bondage, speak the name of Jesus against it: "I am doing all things in the name of Jesus!"

That is how you keep from being entangled again in a yoke. We saw how bondage is actually an area of death. But John 20:31 tells you that in Jesus' name is life:

"...believe that Jesus is the Christ, the Son of God; and that believing you might have life through His name" (John 20:31).

Have you been bowed down? Then Jesus wants to be the lifter of your head. He wants to set you free—but He also wants to **keep** you free, and He can keep you free when you live according to the power of His name.

ANOINTING

Old Testament leaders such as priests and kings were set apart for their God-given positions through ceremonies which included the anointing of oil. The oil was symbolic of the Holy Spirit's impartation of His ability to fulfill the task to which God had appointed them.

God has a special anointing which will fill you with that same ability to live free of bondages by breaking their grip in your life:

> *"And it shall come to pass in that day, that his burden shall be taken away from off thy shoulder, and his yoke from off thy neck, and the yoke shall be destroyed because of the anointing"* (Isaiah 10:27).

There is a special anointing of liberty which wells up inside and flows out of those who spend a part of each day praying in the Spirit. I have never met anyone who has overdone praying in the Spirit, but I have met those who don't do it enough. Imagine the results we would see in every church service if all believers first spent an hour praying in the Spirit. What would happen? They would bring the anointing with them to change lives.

In such a service, unbelievers would come under immediate conviction because the presence of the Holy Spirit would be so strong. They would fall under God's power in repentance, or flood the aisles: "I cannot wait. Tell me what must I do to be saved?"

There is freedom in the anointing which comes through praying in the Spirit. But first dedicate yourself to letting the anointing touch your life before you expect it to touch the lives of others.

THE YOKE OF SERVICE

While Jesus wants you to be free from yokes of bondage, it was never His plan for you to be hanging loose, going nowhere, unaware of any responsibility. As His disciple, you have to commit every area of your life that He reveals to you, and this is really a process. As you grow, He will show you new commitments that you are to make. Yes, Jesus has a yoke for you. It is not a yoke of bondage, but it is a yoke of discipleship.

I am always seeing Christians wearing necklaces or rings with the symbol of a cross on them to show others the mark of their faith. But to this day, I haven't yet seen a Christian wearing a necklace with the symbol of a yoke, have you? The cross is an apt symbol because it is there that your Christian life begins: you take up your cross and follow the Lord Jesus Christ. But Jesus' yoke is where your Christian life continues.

He said, *"Take my yoke upon you, and learn of me; for I am meek and lowly in heart: and ye shall find rest unto your souls. For my yoke is easy, and my burden is light"* (Matthew 11:29,30).

Why are some Christians so unsettled and so restless? It is because they have not allowed themselves to come under Jesus' yoke of authority. They are fearful that being yoked to Jesus Christ means that they must give something up. But Jesus said, "If you take my yoke you will have rest in your soul." When you give yourself wholly to Him, He gives you rest and peace in return. The most unhappy Christians I know are the ones who are trying to walk in the middle of the road.

Notice that Jesus said, *"Take my yoke upon you and learn of me."* When you accept His yoke and start learning of Him in His Word, suddenly His burden becomes your burden: to carry out and live by the Word of God. His desires become your desires.

You will never fear the bondage of sin when you are carrying the burden of His Word. The yoke of the law will never weight you down, for you will be walking by love; and you will be equally yoked to Him in the balance of His Word and agreement with believers.

A friend once asked me to pray for a man whom he referred to as "my spiritual father." It was so precious to me when he said, "This man is very depressed—but he will not stay that way!"

How could he say that? Because he had yoked himself to another believer. He was telling me, "I'm walking with him. I'm standing for him, and he'll come through to victory because I won't let go."

Be willing to yoke yourself to other believers, and to carry the Word for them when they are weak. Yoke them to yourself, and stand in the gap for them. It isn't always easy. It can be wearying to try to walk with someone who has fallen down. But if you won't let go, they cannot stay down.

God wants you free from bondage for one reason: to help others in the Body of Christ be set free. Cast off bondages by taking the yoke of commitment to Jesus Christ upon yourself. It's a commitment of love; that's why it is easy, and that's why it is light.

Chapter 2

FREEDOM FROM FEAR

Fear. It is the enemy whom Christ came into this world to conquer. Fear is the spirit from whom we have been delivered, so that we can walk according to the spirit of liberty. Peter had a terrible fear, which ultimately led him straight into the denial of Christ. Discover how deliverance from the fear of death will crush all fear from your life entirely.

Fear is the Christian's most dangerous enemy. In the Hebrew language, fear is described as "a life long attendant." How fitting, for in the world fear is a very real companion, like it or not. It is no wonder that in Romans, Paul said that Jesus Christ delivered us who were **all our lives** subject to fear of death. Jesus delivered us from the fear that would otherwise have been our "life long attendant."

But as a Christian you probably know that fear still creeps in at times. Fear attacks us today as it attacked Jesus' disciples when they walked with Him on this earth. Why else would Jesus have continually said, "Fear not. Fear not. Fear not."? He acknowledged that fear was indeed a very real threat to faith; and that is why He wants to set us free from it.

In following chronologically through Peter's life I found a pattern of fear that is too often very real for Christians. His life is an example of how fear does not always disappear overnight; but it shows the restorative process that Christ wants to create in all of us. By maturing in His divine restoration, you discover how to not only get free from fear, but to stay free from it.

Don't get me wrong; just because Peter allowed fear to grip him at times, that doesn't discount his faith. It's just that many times his faith was based on a zeal that somehow focused outside of God's Word. But there were moments during his discipleship when his faith showed revelation beyond that of any other of Christ's disciples. For instance in Matthew 16:15, Jesus asked Peter, *"Who do you say that I am?"* Peter's marvelous answer is the profoundest truth of the New Testament:

"And Simon Peter answered and said, Thou art

the Christ, the Son of the Living God" (Matthew 16:16).

Jesus knew that Peter didn't get that knowledge through his natural senses. He said, *"Blessed are you Simon Barjona: for flesh and blood hath not revealed it unto thee, but my Father which is in heaven. And I say also unto thee, That thou art Peter, and upon this rock I will build my church; and the gates of hell shall not prevail against it"* (Matthew 16:17-18).

Before he was ever converted, Peter received revelation from the Spirit of God! Jesus said, "Your **statement** (Thou art Christ. . . .) is one which my Church will be built upon."

Jesus did not build His church on Peter; He built it on the revelation of His deity, the acknowledgement that He is Lord.

Looking further on in Peter's life, however, you will find that not all was faith to faith. A matter of months after having made the greatest statement that a man could make, Peter made the worst statement: he denied knowing Jesus at all. How could a man be so extreme? He did the best—and he did the worst.

Have you ever felt that way? You've confessed the Word and had your greatest victory; then five hours later you really blow it. You wonder, "Oh, God, how could I do it?"

If you understand how this extreme conflict, motivated by fear, occurred in Peter's life, you won't allow it to happen in yours. Matthew 26:74 shows this dark moment of denial:

"Then began he to curse and to swear, saying, I

know not the man. . . ."

Is that the same man who said, "Thou art Christ, the Son of the living God"? That's Peter. Now he says, "I don't know Him!"

How did Peter get himself into this position of denial? I know what is behind it: fear. Jesus had been his intimate Friend, Guide, and Counselor for three years. Now He had been taken away for trial and judgment, and Peter was afraid that he also would be taken and tried. When the Lord's enemies recognized Peter they said, "You've been with that Galilean; you're one of His disciples."

Peter abhorred the thought of crucifixion. He was filled with fear and he began cursing and swearing. Out of terror for his own life, Peter denied knowing his Lord.

Peter didn't just suddenly come into this fear, however. I have seen that fear is very subtle, and it is a very gradual process. Just as when you begin reading God's Word and grow in revelation knowledge, you can also regress in a process of fear. Faith will take you from strength to strength and glory to glory; fear will take you into growing weakness until it manifests itself in sin.

I want you to look at Peter's life to see how he started with one statement of fear, and eventually found himself in its control. His first real mistake with fear— strangely enough—happened immediately after he made the tremendous statement, "Thou art the Christ, the Son of the living God."

After Peter confessed Christ's Lordship, Jesus began

explaining to His disciples that he would have to die on the cross and be resurrected. Peter could not imagine losing his Lord, and he reacted violently:

"Then Peter took him, and began to rebuke him, saying, Be it far from thee, Lord: this shall not be unto thee. But he turned, and said unto Peter, Get thee behind me, Satan: thou art an offence unto me: for thou savourest not the things that be of God, but those that be of men" (Matthew 16:22,23).

Some people will excuse Peter's reaction: "He made this statement out of a right heart."

But you can be sincere and still be sincerely wrong. We have too often lifted up sincerity as the ultimate measuring rod: "As long as he is sincere, it's all right."

Just remember that a criminal is sincere in his crimes. Sincerity alone does not make a person right; rather, you have to be sincere about the Truth, which is God's Word. Peter was not looking at God's Word when he made this statement. He was looking at his fears.

Jesus had given Peter the words of truth for three years. He had been the Shepherd, the Messiah Whom the prophets had spoken of. Now He said, "I'm leaving," and it shook Peter's soul.

"No, Jesus! I won't let this happen."

Can you imagine telling Jesus what to do? He was The Truth, and here was Peter saying, "You're wrong."

Peter's first step towards really blowing it was by denying the cross of Jesus Christ. Why did he do it? Was it out of compassion for Jesus? No, it stemmed from fear.

He's been thinking, "We've found the Son of God, the Messiah. He's ours. He's going to deliver us from Roman rule and we're going to rule and reign with Him."

But he could not see this simple truth: that before the crown must come the cross. As far as Peter was concerned, anything having to do with the cross would put the crown away. How could Messiah establish His rule if He died? No way. Peter's first fear was a fear of the cross.

That fear still exists today, because inherent in the human personality is also a struggle with the fear of the cross. We are so fearful about having to die to our own desires. We so often fall short of willingness to say, "Jesus, I am willing to surrender all to Your cross."

That unwillingness to surrender our old nature is fear. Paul had a revelation that we must "die" at the cross by faith:

> *"I am crucified with Christ: nevertheless I live; yet not I, but Christ liveth in me: and the life which I now live in the flesh I live by the faith of the Son of God, who loved me, and gave himself for me" (Galatians 2:20).*

Whether you like it or not, you must be willing to crucify a lot of the hidden corners of your life. You've got to allow the Holy Spirit to shine His searchlight through your soul and show you how to crucify those dark areas. The fear of allowing our old nature to die is a deceiver, for before the crown must come the cross. The cross is a place of victory, not a place of fear.

But Peter was blind to the truth about Jesus' crucifixion and that He had to die before He could bring life. Fear had entered in, and it began popping up all over the place. He made one negative statement, and then he found himself making more of them. Matthew 26:31-35 shows that Peter was still not seeing God's Word because he began boasting in himself. And when you start saying, "It's **my** strength accomplishing this," you're in trouble. As he discovered later, confidence in the flesh always brings a big letdown.

> *"Then saith Jesus unto them, All ye shall be offended because of me this night: for it is written, I will smite the shepherd, and the sheep of the flock shall be scattered abroad. But after I am risen again, I will go before you into Galilee. Peter answered and said unto him, Though all men shall be offended because of thee, yet will I never be offended . . . Though I should die with thee, yet will I not deny thee. . . ." (Matthew 26:31-35).*

What is Peter doing? He is saying, "Oh Jesus, the rest of the disciples may be offended because of You. But I would never do that. I would die with You first."

Have you ever heard other believers exalt their own strength in this way? They'll tell you, "Have you heard about so-and-so? They really blew it, but I would never dream of doing what they did."

That is nothing more than confidence in the flesh. You can say, "Jesus in me is greater than he that is in the world." You can say, "I can do all things through Christ Who strengthens me."

Confidence in God's Word will always keep you and bring you through during a trial. But Peter's misplaced assurance in his own ability is what failed him. You see, fear brings you to a point where you rely on your own courage and bravery: "I'll be brave! I'll be brave!" But the characteristics of true bravery and courage aren't found in the flesh; they are only found in the Spirit.

Then in Mark 14:47 you see Peter getting into a really zealous spirit; but it is not Word-inspired. Again, I see it tying into his inner fear of the cross; he just cannot bear thinking about Jesus going to the cross because that spoils all of his plans. So when the Jews came to take Jesus away, Peter was overtaken with a spirit of fear, and it drove him into a wrong zeal in his own motives:

"And one of them that stood by drew a sword, and smote a servant of the high priest, and cut off his ear."

He's trying to help Jesus avoid the cross! Oh, that fear was just chewing on Peter, and it was starting to show up in his conduct. Jesus was led away, and Peter followed Him. But in what way did he follow? The Bible says that he was now **afar off.** Fear puts a distance between you and your Lord because it deteriorates your trust. Oh, you're following Him, but there becomes a distance because you are relying on personal works, not on faith.

How did Peter get so far away from Jesus? It started with his first statement, "I'll never let you go to the cross." It ended up with, "I'll die before you go to the cross; I'll cut off people's ears before you go to the cross."

Then in Mark 14:66, Peter's fear reached its peak:

"And as Peter was beneath in the palace, there cometh one of the maids of the high priest: And

31

when she saw Peter warming himself, she looked upon him, and said, And thou also wast with Jesus of Nazareth" (14:66,67).

"You were with Jesus! You were His follower."

Peter denied it. He denied it again. And finally when they said, "We can tell you're one of His by the way you speak," what did Peter do? He began to curse, and to swear. He said, "I don't know him!"

As he spoke those words, a cock crowed in the distance and the Words of his Lord came rushing back, *"before the cock crow, thou shalt deny me thrice"* (Matthew 26:34). Peter was now flooded with guilt and sorrow.

You say, "Well, he was afraid!"

But fear never justifies wrong deeds; it only creates them. It begins as a seedling, and soon it brings companions of condemnation and sorrow. All of this denial began with a seedling of fear: the fear of the cross, implanting itself into Peter's soul. Now it had saturated all of his actions.

Fear of losing Jesus, fear of having to die for his faith, fear of losing his security blinded Peter to the victory of the cross. Fear never respects the things of God because it is a deceiver.

But in the midst of this dark picture, I also found the steps of restoration that Jesus planted. What happens when Jesus plants the Word? It never returns void. Jesus always wants to help us overcome fear, and you overcome it by applying to your life the same process He applied to Peter.

First of all, Jesus used prayer against fear:

"And the Lord said, Simon, Simon, behold, Satan hath desired to have you that he may sift you as wheat: But I have prayed for thee, that thy faith fail not: and when thou art converted, strengthen thy brethren" (Luke 22:31,32).

Have you ever looked for the places when Jesus called Peter, "Simon?" Why would He revert to Peter's old name which He had originally changed? I discovered that the Bible reveals four occasions when Jesus called him, "Simon," and there is a specific reason for it.

One of the connotations for the word "Simon" is "hearing." So whenever Jesus used that name He was saying, "Be a hearing one; I have a message for you."

Upon first calling Peter to be a fisher of men, Jesus called out, "Simon!" He was saying, "Hear your call!"

When Peter revealed that Jesus was the Christ, Jesus' reply was, "Simon, flesh and blood didn't reveal this to you." He said, "You've been **hearing** from God."

Now He is focusing Peter's attention on God's Word: "Although you will know Satan's attempts to sift your faith, LISTEN: I've prayed for you. Remember: I've prayed for you."

You say, "His faith did fail."

No, it did not fail. Peter's courage failed him, and that is why we must be cautious about where we place our reliance. Our own courage will never be enough. Peter's courage failed him; but his faith did not fail. After he denied Jesus he wept bitterly; he still believed.

Sometimes you may feel as though you really failed, and the devil will lie to you, "Why bother trying again? You can't do it."

But although you may have blown it, you may have said wrong things, done wrong things, and faltered in courage, hold on to Him. Your faith will not fail you, and it will hold you up if your bravery lets you down.

Your first step out of fear is in knowing that Jesus has prayed for you, and that He still prays for you. In John 17:20 before His death Jesus prayed to His Father and in that prayer He said, *"Neither pray I for these alone, but for them also which shall believe on me through their word; . . ."*

Then in Hebrews 7:25 it says that Jesus "ever liveth to make intercession for us." He prayed for you then. He's praying for you now. When you hit fear you can say, "Satan's trying to sift me; but my faith won't fail because Jesus is making intercession for me to come through." Amen

Then in Luke 22:61 you find the second step of restoration. When Peter was busily denying his relationship to Jesus, Who should come by and see him, but the very Man he is denying. Oh, can you imagine having just cursed and sworn and denied your Lord, when suddenly you look up and there He is looking at you? As Peter says, "I don't know Him," verse 61 says, *"and the Lord turned and looked upon Peter."*

When you read that, you can almost feel the piercing of Jesus' eyes. I found the definition of the word "look," and it does not mean simply "to look upon." It means "to look through." Jesus looked **through** Peter. What do you suppose that look said? Was He saying, "Peter, you are letting Me down when I need you the most. You said you would die for Me, but now you are cursing Me."

No, I don't believe Jesus' look said that at all. I believe that He was looking through to Peter's soul and saying, "Oh, Peter, don't do this to yourself."

So the second part of knowing what to do when fear strikes is to remember that Jesus **sees** you. He isn't condemning you, He wants to help. He sees you right where you are, and He still loves you.

Jesus also has a third step of restoration from fear, and it is shown after His resurrection. Remember, the last look Peter had from Jesus before His death was the one after he denied Him. Then after Jesus' resurrection from death, Mary and her sister Salome visited the sepulchre with the intent of anointing Jesus' body for burial. The stone had been rolled away from the tomb, and as they entered the sepulchre, they saw a man sitting on the right side. He spoke to them:

> *And he saith unto them, Be not affrighted: Ye seek Jesus of Nazareth, which was crucified: he is risen; he is not here: behold the place where they laid him. But go your way, tell his disciples and Peter that he goeth before you into Galilee: . . ." (Mark 16:6,7a).*

Why didn't he just say, "Tell His disciples that He is going before you to Galilee"? Why "and Peter"?

Because Jesus wanted Peter to have a personal message of His love. "Peter, I'm not angry. I know that you cursed and denied me. I know that you followed me from afar. I know that you cut off the high priest's ear and I had to perform one of My last miracles because you got carried away. But the cross was right for Me all along; and I have risen for you."

"Tell my disciples—and Peter," He said. Have you

ever noticed that in a heavy attack of fear, Jesus will give you a personal message through His Word? Once, during a trial where the natural circumstances were almost impossible to bear, I called out to God for a personal message: "God, I must have something fresh from You. I know that I claim these daily Scriptures, but I need something straight from You."

He gave me the most precious Scripture from the book of Haggai, and I still use it against fear today:

"According to the word I covenanted with you when ye came out of Egypt, so my spirit remaineth among you: fear ye not" (Haggai 2:5).

Jesus has a personal message for you in His Word. It's not just "God's Word for Christians." It's for you. Then in 1 Corinthians 15:5 I saw that not only did Jesus send Peter a personal message, but He also had a personal meeting with him directly after His resurrection:

"And that he was seen of Cephas, then of the twelve: . . ." (1 Corinthians 15:5).

I always imagined Jesus' appearance to the disciples in the locked room as His first. But Jesus went right to Peter before He ever talked to the rest of His disciples. He wanted to say, "Peter, I still love you. I prayed for you, I saw you, I sent you a message—and you're coming through."

There are times when Jesus wants personal interviews with you. He wants you to come and refresh yourself, waiting in His presence. He wants to talk with you, and with you alone.

Have you ever awakened in the night with fear flooding in through every fiber of your soul, when the warmth of Jesus' presence comes to drive it away? Those personal moments with Jesus will dissipate any fear surrounding you; He wants to calm the storm within, and that is why He promised, "I'll never leave you nor forsake you."

These quiet times alone with Jesus are carved from God's love, especially for your reassurance. Jesus' personal presence is as much yours as is His Word.

Jesus is not angry with people who are fearful. He's praying for them, wanting to bring them out of it. So when you see people who are surrounded by fear, don't get frustrated with them. If they're not in faith, share yours. Don't put them down, lift them up. Jesus in you has something for them, doesn't He? He has restoration-resurrection power.

Now that these steps toward pulling Peter out of fear had taken place, Jesus still had to deal directly with what happened. You say, "He still loves me."

That is true; but He still has to deal directly with the fear. It isn't enough to say, "It's all right, honey. You were only afraid."

Don't baby your fears. Fear is Satan's device to quench your faith and turn you into an ineffective Christian. Sympathy has never been the answer to ridding the devil of his weapons in your life. Jesus dealt with Peter right where he was, and the way He totally delivered him from fear is dynamite!

"After these things Jesus shewed himself again to the disciples at the sea of Tiberias; and on this wise shewed he himself. There were together Simon Peter, and Thomas called Didymus, and

Nathanael of Cana in Galilee, and the sons of Zebedee, and two other of his disciples. Simon saith unto them, I go a fishing'' (John 21:1-3a).

The Greek translation for Peter's statement is, ''I am returning to the fishing trade.''

Peter isn't just taking a little vacation; he is going back to his old life. Why is he going back? Jesus prayed for him. He's had a personal meeting with him, yet he wants to go back? ''Why?'' I wondered.

It is because Peter's spiritual eyes are still perceiving the cross as a place of defeat. He feels as though he was let down, and the idea of Jesus' death on the cross still gnaws on his mind. Not only did he decide to return to the old fishing trade, as a leader he influenced six other disciples to go along. So they set out on a ship, but they didn't even catch a guppy that night!

When the morning came, there was Jesus standing on the shore, and the disciples failed to recognize Him. He called out to them in the boat:

''. . . *Children have ye any meat? They answered him, No'' (John 21:5).*

Jesus used a fascinating word for ''children.'' The interpretation of the word is similar to ''pedagogue,'' which is a child under tutoring. In other words Jesus was saying, ''**Students**: I am teaching you something!''

When they said, ''We have caught nothing,'' He instructed them, ''Then cast your net over the right side of the ship. There you will find fish.''

I could understand the disciples obeying that command if they knew that the stranger on the shore was Jesus. But they still had not recognized Him, so why did they follow through with the instruction? In studying this out, I saw that often you can pinpoint the location of great schools of fish by where the water of a lake is darkened. Sometimes on the sea of Galilee, men would be appointed to stand on the shore and direct the fishermen to where the darkened waters were. The disciples, expecting to find a school of fish, cast their net over the right side of the ship, and there were so many fish! Verse six says, *"They were not able to draw it for the multitude of fishes."*

The strength of seven disciples together was not enough to pull in this great net full of fish. At this moment, John looked up and saw His Lord standing on the shore. He knew what was going on, for he recognized Jesus.

When Peter heard that Jesus was on the shore, he grabbed his coat and leaped off the boat to swim ashore. (That sounds just like Peter; he was always doing something impulsive.) The rest of the disciples rowed the boat in, and it couldn't have been easy because they were dragging along this tremendous catch of fish. When they came to land, here is what happened:

"As soon as they were come to land, they saw a fire of coals there, and fish laid thereon, and bread. Jesus saith unto them, Bring of the fish which ye have now caught. Simon Peter went up, and drew the net to land full of great fishes, . . ." (John 21:9,10,11a).

One man, Simon Peter, managed to drag the entire net of fish to the shore all by himself. Why is it that seven of them couldn't muster the strength to draw in the net—but one man did it alone? It is because after

Peter had received a vision and a touch from Jesus, he received strength. Once you get a vision of Jesus, nothing is the same again; you can do all things through Christ Who strengthens you.

Now Jesus was going to deal with him. Notice that when the disciples came to the land, Jesus had a fire burning. Peter thought, "I remember the last fire I warmed myself near; it was when I denied You."

Jesus had that fire ready on purpose. He wanted to heal those memories of the enemy's fire by allowing Peter to warm himself over the fire of a Friend Who is closer than a brother. Then, did Jesus call Peter into the humiliation of a public scene? Did He say, "Peter, I want to bring up everything that you did wrong"?

No, instead he prepared food to strengthen Peter's tired body after a difficult and discouraging night. We always tend to downplay the importance of physical needs: "On the scope of eternity, what's a physical need?"

The needs of His cold, tired, hungry disciples were very important to Jesus. He met those needs first. Then he said it: "**Simon.**"

Oh dear! There is that name again, and He's getting ready with a message. Jesus said, "Simon Peter (are you listening?), do you love Me more than these?"

These what? These fish. "Do you love Me more than this fishing trade of yours?"

"Oh, yes, Lord, You know that I love You."

The word that Jesus used in asking whether Peter loved Him was "Agape," and it is a love that gives without expecting in return. Peter's answer was one

40

which said, "I don't have that Agape love. But I love You with a reciprocal love; You are my friend."

Peter is so honest, isn't he? He answered the Lord's question, and Jesus said, "Feed my lambs."

The word "feed" means "Give the young disciples the best of nourishment."

Jesus asked him again, "Simon, do you love (agape) Me?"

Simon said, "Lord, You know that I love (phileo) You. You know what kind of love I have for You—because You know me."

Jesus replied, "Feed my sheep," using a different word for "feed." It means, "train and discipline." Notice that Jesus is not speaking of lambs, but sheep. Given the best of nourishment, the disciples mature into the ability to receive training and direction.

But now Jesus looked at Simon and asked him, "Simon, son of Jonas. Do you love (phileo) Me? Do you even love Me as a Friend?"

And Peter's heart wrenched; he was grieved. "Oh, Jesus, do you even doubt my reciprocal love for You?" Then, "Lord, You know all things, including my love for You."

Now came the calling, "Feed my sheep," meaning "Nourish these older ones with fine nourishment." The Lord has called Simon Peter from being a fisher of men, to a teacher of sheep. "Nourish and love them; nourish and love them."

When I looked at this scene and imagined it, I found it interesting that Peter professed his love for Jesus three times—exactly as many times as he had denied Him.

41

Within those confessions came the warmth of healing and restoration. From the restoration came the call: Feed my sheep.

Now Jesus probed into the exact place from where Peter's fear had originated:

"Verily, verily, I say unto thee, When thou wast young, thou girdest thyself, and walkedst whither thou wouldest: but when thou shalt be old, thou shalt stretch forth thy hands, and another shall gird thee, and carry thee whither thou wouldest not. This spake he, signifying by what death he should glorify God. And when he had spoken this, he saith unto him, Follow me" *(John 21:18,19).*

Jesus was saying, "I know your fear; I know that you have been fearing the cross all along."

Peter was martyred on a cross, and Jesus told him about it before it ever happened. Historians say that when Peter was crucified, he refused to die in the same manner as his Lord; he cried, "I am not worthy." He was crucified upside-down.

Talk about somebody moving right in and taking the fear. If someone came and told me that I would be crucified, my first thought would be, "I'll never go to another foreign country."

But Jesus brought Peter to such complete deliverance that he was willing to go anyway. It didn't matter to him, because suddenly he saw that the cross was a place of victory: first the cross, and then the crown. I believe that Jesus was saying, "Peter, you won't be fearful, because I'll be there to take you right out of it."

Then look at what Peter said—he is so funny. He turned and saw John, "the disciple who Jesus loved," standing nearby and he said, "Lord, and what shalt this man do?"

Reading that you just want to say, "Oh, Peter. . . ."

Jesus told him, "If I will that he tarries until I come back, why do you care? Follow Me; just keep your eyes on Me."

Not only did Jesus completely restore Peter from his fear of the cross, not only did He forgive all of his faults, but He brought him back into the ministry he was called to fulfill.

He said, "Now get out of fish and get with sheep." Once He said, "You'll fish for men." Now He said, "You'll feed them."

Did Peter change? If you think that he had fear problems afterward, you're mistaken. In Acts 2:14, he was a changed man:

> *"But Peter, standing up with the eleven, lifted up his voice, and said unto them, Ye men of Judaea, and all ye that dwell in Jerusalem, . . ."*

He preached a sermon that wouldn't stop! They could have killed him, but he didn't care; instead, "Jesus, Jesus, Jesus," was the message that he preached and 3,000 men were converted that day! Is that the Peter of fear? No, that is the Peter who was restored by the hand of the Lord Himself.

When you study the epistles of Paul, do you remember that one time he had to correct Peter? He said, "Quit acting holier than thou! Get with the program."

But in reading 1 and 2 Peter, he has a different character than the Peter of fear may have displayed. He is such a man of God that he already lives at the cross and his old man is dead. About Paul he writes, "Our beloved brother, Paul."

He'd been to the cross, and dead men don't scream, do they? Dead men aren't offended, are they? If your flesh is offended it is because you haven't left it at the cross. You're afraid of the cross, but it's supposed to be your place of victory, because that is where your fear died.

Be a Simon and dismiss fear when it comes your way: be a hearing one. Jesus did not come to give us fear; He came to deliver us from it. Psalms 112:7 speaks of the fearless man: *"He shall not be afraid of evil tidings: his heart is fixed, trusting in the Lord."*

When Peter heard Jesus say, "Follow me," he fixed his heart and never looked back. Instead of fear, he had boldness.

Be bold! Let your flesh and your fears die at the cross and start living in the resurrection life of Jesus Christ. Jesus took Peter right to the cross and delivered him from fear; He wants you to get your deliverance at the cross also. First the cross, then the crown. Peter never feared again, and you don't have to either.

Chapter 3

FREEDOM IN TESTS AND TRIALS

Do you ever really feel like "counting it all joy" when you run head-on into a fiery trial? Not really...and especially not when the enemy comes to you with temptation. Here's how to have freedom to walk in the Spirit and resist temptation even in the severest of tests or trials.

I hear so many Christians expound on the joys of going "From strength to strength, faith to faith, and glory to glory!"

Yet I seldom hear about the test or trial that stimulated them to grow from one level of maturity to the next. Tests and trials are something that we don't like to think about; but chances are as you read this you are in the middle of some type of a test. You probably have your faith out for some provision in some area of your life; and when the answer to your faith is revealed, again you will have moved from one strength to another strength.

Life for the Christian is one of joy, peace and love. But I have also heard it described as a series of tests and trials which stimulate us to further growth.

You say, "How do you know I'm in a test?"

Because it takes one to know one. I've been through many tests, and I expect to go through many more. But there is nothing wrong with a test. In fact, they can have a very positive impact on your life. For instance, if you passed a test in school you would be promoted into a higher level. The same principle applies to you: God wants to promote you through the tests that you face in your life.

I believe that God may actually bring tests your way, but He will never bring anything that you are not ready for. He only wants to prove and strengthen your faith; He does not want you to fail. But Genesis 22:1 says that God "tempted" Abraham. Does God want to tempt you? Look at the passage of Scripture:

"And it came to pass after these things, that God

did tempt Abraham, and said unto him, Abraham: and he said, Behold, here I am. And he said, Take now thy son, thine only son Isaac, whom thou lovest, and get thee into the land of Moriah; and offer him there for a burnt offering upon one of the mountains which I will tell thee of" (Genesis 22:1,2).

This passage describes the moment when God asked Abraham to sacrifice that which was most precious to him: his son of promise. The account distinctly says that **God Tempted Abraham**—yet most Christians are also familiar with James 1:13, which says, *"Let no man say when he is tempted, I am tempted of God: for God cannot be tempted with evil, neither tempteth he any man:..."*

I have heard skeptics of the Bible say, "Oh, it's full of contradictions."

Is that right? The only reason they say that is because they've never read it or taken the time to study it for themselves. You see, the Hebrew word for "tempt" is the word **nacah,** meaning "to prove," or "try."

If I was going to **prove** a point, I would have to believe in what I was saying, wouldn't I? In the same way, God was saying, "Abraham, I know that you already have the faith; I just want to prove it to you. It will make you stronger, and that way I can give you a greater miracle."

So although God may give us some tests, He will never tempt us. Only the devil will tempt, and he will do so with a vengeance. Never think that you're exempt from temptation. Jesus was tempted in every way as we are: and if he was tempted, you can expect the same.

There is a big difference between temptation and testing: it is that tests are on the outside, but temptation is on the inside. Tests will involve difficulties in some type of sensory area of your life; while a temptation is an attack on your soul. When you are struggling with how to handle some sort of a test in your life, be instantly aware that the devil wants to use this time to hit you with temptation. He doesn't want you to have victory over trials; he wants just the opposite!

Because God knew that temptations would come during tests or trials, He provided you with keys in His Word telling you how to respond. God has a strategy in mind for you during a test: He wants to bring you a miracle greater than if the trial had not come.

In Abraham's test, before he got the miracle, you can be sure that he was tempted to doubt God. A lot of us tend to rationalize, "Oh, Abraham was the great man of faith! He would have sacrificed his son!"

But those of us who are parents understand that burning love you have for your child. You would die for that child, if necessary; and yet here Abraham was being asked to give the child's life. He may have thought, "Oh, God, why not my life instead?"

The devil could have told him, "God is much too hard on you. He isn't merciful, or He would never have asked you to sacrifice your son."

Abraham may have been tempted to compromise. He may have thought, "Oh, I'll obey God, but I'll bring a sacrifice lamb along—just in case!"

But remember that Abraham had been walking with God for many years. He knew from experience that tests and trials are God's opportunities to bring miracles—and our opportunities to trust Him for them. In any case, he made a right decision. He said, "God, even if You have to resurrect my son from the dead, I know that you are faithful. You won't go back on Your promise."

What happened? God gave Abraham a revelation of the Messiah who would be a Light to nations on that same mountain range. Abraham spoke of Jesus:

> *"And Abraham called the name of that place Jehovah-jireh: as it is said to this day, In the mount of the Lord it shall be seen" (Genesis 22:14).*

On that day, God said, "Because you did not withhold your only son, I will not withhold Mine." And then he made a covenant with Abraham. Why? Because Abraham made a right decision in a test: He decided to obey God.

When you know God wants to promote you in faith by giving you a miracle, suddenly a test seems less trying. Then you will make a right decision. God is no respecter of persons. He has miracles for you in your tests just as He did for Abraham, because you're Abraham's seed by faith.

Don't think that God is looking down and thinking, "What kind of a test can I put on her?"

No, He first wants to strengthen your faith until you are ready; but there comes a time when you must act according to what you know. A lot of Christians today get so much teaching, and yet they do nothing with it. They're still sick, they're still complaining about everything. Why? Because they won't do something with the bit God has given them.

In the case of the Israelites, God gave them a lot to go on before He expected them to act in faith. He gave them ten major miracles before they even left Egypt with Moses. Ten severe plagues devastated the Egyptians and their land, yet never came near or touched the Israelites. God showed His power mightily.

Then they had an eleventh miracle immediately after they left Egypt when God parted the Red Sea. It was as though God was saying, "I was with you there and I'm still with you! I am guiding you."

By that time I would have imagined that the children of Israel would almost get excited when a test came: "What's God going to do now!"

But faced with a trial only a day or two after the Red Sea miracle, it is distressing to say that the Israelites still refused to look at God in a trial. Only one day later, when they found themselves parched and without water, they started wondering, "Where is God? I thought He was with us, but apparently not."

The threat of dying of thirst in the wilderness was certainly a troublesome one. There were over a million people, so you can imagine the sound of children and babies crying, not to mention the animals that needed water.

Soon, another day had passed miserably by, and the people began to feel desperate. "Moses, you brought us here to die!" they accused their leader.

When they finally found water, their great joy was short-lived, finding out that the water was completely unsuitable for drinking!

"And when they came to Marah, they could not

drink of the waters of Marah, for they were bitter:...'' (Exodus 15:23a).

Think of the disappointment. I thought, "Lord, it would be worse finding water that you cannot drink, than to find no water at all." In their frustration, the people turned all of their hostility on Moses, and the Bible tells us how he handled it:

"And the people murmured against Moses, saying, what shall we drink? And he cried unto the Lord; and the Lord shewed him a tree, which when he had cast into the waters, the waters were made sweet:..." (Exodus 15:24,25).

He cried to the Lord. He didn't yell at the people, or start having a big pity party. He said, "God, every one of these people wants to kill me, but I know that you have a miracle for all of us."

He could have said, "You don't deserve a miracle!" couldn't he have? But because Moses looked to God for the answer, God gave him a way to sweeten the waters—for **everyone** concerned. He doesn't sit up in heaven with a stick, hoping for a chance to wipe people out; He's looking for one person to stand in the gap for everyone else. He has a miracle for your trial.

Then the Lord showed me, "During that trial, all of those people's trust was not in Me; it was in finding water." They thought, "If we find water, that will quench our thirst." But the water they found was bitter, and it proves something: we often think we know the answer to our problem. We think, "I need this!" and we go after it. But if we go after God, instead of a material answer, then the provision will always be sweet. If we don't, sometimes what we thought we needed can really end up tasting bitter! Seek the Lord, not the material provision. When you do, He'll bring you the provision that is tailor-made to fill the area of need.

The people were looking to water as their source of life—and the water let them down because it was bitter. But Moses looked to God, and that day in the wilderness a million people came through to victory because of what one man did. You have a choice: to murmur, or to speak God's Word. But only one of those choices will get you the miracle!

Sometimes we want to keep God in a mental "box" that says. "This is how He'll answer my prayer." But when we do so, we limit Him. It isn't until we look totally to Him that He can bring the miracle. I learned this by experience, in the early years of full-time ministry.

I was scheduled to speak at a luncheon in Buffalo, New York, but because of a storm, the plane couldn't land in Buffalo. We were flown to Rochester and told that we would be bussed into the city. It began to appear that I would be seriously late for the speaking engagement. I asked, "What time will we be in Buffalo?"

They said, "Oh, around 2:30."

Inside I panicked; that would make me an hour and a half late! I couldn't make a phone call, so the devil really used the opportunity to attack my imagination: "Oh, you'll get there, and they'll all be gone."

"That's the last speaking engagement you'll ever get."

Then the bus driver was really taking the scenic route—I'd never been on a bus this slow. It was so frustrating, and I really just wanted to gripe all over the place, but suddenly God just checked me in my spirit. He said, "Do you believe that I can bring a miracle out of this?"

That's when you say, "All right, God. I'll trust you."

Did I arrive on time? No, I was as late as had been predicted. By this time you really tend to think, "Where is the miracle?"

As I walked in the large luncheon and conference hall, a woman I had never met in my life came running over. She said, "I'm so glad you are here! You won't believe the strange thing that happened. We were supposed to begin the luncheon at noon; but the hotel made a mistake, and didn't book us until 1:30. We're just finishing the luncheon now, and you're exactly on time."

What are tests? They are opportunities for miracles. They are your chance to be still and see the salvation of God. How do you respond in tests and trials? Do you gripe, or do you hang in there to get your miracle from it?

I Peter 4:12 & 13 tell us that there is a reward at the end of a trial:

> "Beloved, think it not strange concerning the fiery trial which is to try you, as though some strange thing happened unto you: But rejoice, inasmuch as ye are partakers of Christ's sufferings; that, when his glory shall be revealed, ye may be glad also with exceeding joy."

He is saying, "You may be going through hardships now; but there's a miracle at the end of it. Hang in there."

Then James 1:2 goes even further. Peter says, "Don't think that your trial is a strange thing." But James says, *"My brethren, count it all joy when ye fall into divers temptations;..."*

Count it all joy?

To be totally honest, it's not always a cinch for me to be overcome with joy when I'm in the middle of a trial. But God says, "Whether you like it or not doesn't matter. If you use the Scripture, it will work for you."

Why be joyful? It is because the joy of the Lord is your strength, and if you ever need strength it's during a trial. You need joy because you need strength to make it through and get your miracle!

But while you're counting it all joy, the devil has a few tricks to lay on the table, too. He is a sneaky one, but he is also stupid enough to have been exposed. The book of James gives you a key of insight into his devices so that you won't fall for them.

"But every man is tempted, when he is drawn away of his own lust, and enticed" (James 1:14).

What is lust? According to the Scriptures, lust is any desire that you have which is inconsistent to God's will. You can know something is inconsistent with His will because it goes against His Word. It takes priority in your life over His Word.

You say, "Is it wrong to have desires?"

No, it is not wrong. You could desire something as innocent as food or sleep, and they might not be wrong. But when you have an uncontrollable desire to eat you become gluttonous. When you have an uncontrollable desire to sleep you become lazy. At that point a desire

55

becomes lust.

Desire is the first place the devil wants to hit you with temptation. Then, once he has sparked that area, he goes after your intellect with **deception.** He wants to get you involved in reasoning against God's Word. When you listen to that sin, what happens? You enter into **disobedience,** and here is the end result:

> *"Then when lust hath conceived, it bringeth forth sin: and sin, when it is finished, bringeth forth death" (James 1:15).*

First is desire, second is deception, third is disobedience, and these three work together to bring death. The devil isn't trying anything new and flashy; it's the very same old idea he used on Eve in the garden. It's been around since the beginning of creation.

When the serpent beguiled Eve, he first attacked her on the desire for food. He said, "Look at that tree. Doesn't the fruit look delicious?"

Eve thought, "Well, God didn't say I couldn't look at the tree, anyway."

But as she gazed at the tree, suddenly that fruit began to appeal to her. It looked tastier than any fruit in the garden. She beheld that sin, she desired that sin, and she was now open to deception. So the devil told her, "If you ate that fruit it would make you like God."

At that moment, lust conceived and it brought forth sin. Eve thought, "I could be even better! I could be just like God."

But she was already like God. She had been made in His image, so why did she not remember? Because she had been beholding that fruit. She listened to the devil's reasoning, and she fell prey to deception. Sin was the result, and it brought the curse of death upon mankind.

You don't have to be deceived. The Bible has ways for you to put barriers up against temptation. When you use them, they shield you from falling into the devil's lies.

Barrier one is found through **looking ahead.** I see this in the story of King David when he committed adultery with Bathsheba. Through one single sin, his whole life ended up in a mess.

Starting one evening when he had neglected to go to battle, but was lounging on the balcony of the palace, David spied a beautiful young woman bathing in a pool outside. Her husband was away at war, so he took advantage of the fact by seducing her.

Sin is as bait with a hook hidden under it. The fish swims around, sees the bait, thinks, "Food!" and he goes after it. When David looked at Bathsheba bathing in the pool, all he saw was the bait. But if he had looked ahead, he would have considered God's judgment for the sin he wanted to commit.

Because he did not consider the hook—death—that comes with sin, he was hooked by it. Bathsheba discovered that she was going to have a baby, and David had her husband killed in battle to keep him from finding out. Then the baby was born very sick, and he died shortly afterward. Death was the end result of David's sin.

If David had looked ahead he would have been shocked! He would have said, "That's too dangerous! I can't get involved in that because death will be the result.''

After looking ahead and seeing judgment, there is another barrier you can put up against sin, and it is found in James 1:17:

"Every good gift and every perfect gift is from above, and cometh down from the Father of lights, with whom is no variableness, neither shadow of turning."

Barrier two is for you to **look around,** and see and proclaim the goodness of God. Before the Israelites entered the Promised Land, God told them, "I am bringing you into a wonderful land. It is full of fruit trees you never planted; there are houses that you didn't build, wells that you did not dig, and vineyards you didn't plant. You will have gold, silver, and great wealth."

In the same way, how many times God blesses us in spite of what we have done—not because of it! When we were born again, we received new life, and the fulfillment of every one of God's promises through Him. In essence, we entered a Promised Land given to us out of God's grace toward us.

As the Israelites went into a ready-made situation, God has not overlooked any provision in your life, either. He has a provision for every need that you may encounter. So when you meet temptation during a trial you can think, "Why give in to that temptation? God has much better things for me."

The devil never had a bargain for anyone. His temptation is arranged so that you will pay, and you will pay dearly. He wants you to keep paying, keep paying, keep paying. While on the other hand, when the Bible says that every good gift "cometh down" from the Father of lights, it means that God's goodness keeps coming, keeps coming, keeps coming. They just don't quit! But which are you going to choose? Look around—the choice is clear.

Eve could have said, "Who needs that fruit tree? I've got thousands of others, God has been so good to me."

And when the devil lied, "You'll be as smart as God," she could have honestly answered, "I already am."

God isn't holding anything back from you! He desires to be a good Father to you—but you've got to let Him be good: you have to stand against temptation!

Some people have physical afflictions which become a lifelong trial. I've seen some Christians who will say this about someone in a physical trial: "Oh, he is so sick; but he is so spiritual! I went to cheer him up, but he ended up cheering me up. What a blessing that sickness is!"

It is true that the affliction is a trial. But what does God want to do in a trial? He wants to bring a miracle to the situation! When I am sick, I don't feel like being sweet and cheerful. In fact, I feel mean. But I find it a lot easier to be sweet-tempered when I know a miracle is on the way! If I say, "This is a test, and God is going to provide me with a miracle," then I can get sweet amazingly fast!

The first two barriers are to look ahead and see judgment, and to look around and see God's goodness. But the third barrier is the most exciting one. You see, in the Old Covenant the Jews could look ahead to see judgment. They could also look around and see God's goodness in their lives.

You say, "They still failed a lot of times."

But God has made a provision for you that they did not have. You see, barrier three gives you a new place to look: you look **within** to the nature of Jesus Christ in you.

> *"Of his own will begat he us with the word of truth, that we should be a kind of firstfruits of his creatures" (James 1:18).*

When I saw the word firstfruits, I thought of the firstfruits which the children of Israel dedicated to God. When they entered the Land of Promise, God was given the first grapes, the first figs, the first grain. All of it was joyfully gathered, and brought with thanksgiving to the tabernacle. Then the people would praise God and say, "This is the best we have, God. And it's Yours."

Since you are His firstfruits, according to James 1:18, God is looking at you and saying, "You are the best! You have My nature within."

The Old Covenant fell short of offering a third barrier. But in the New Covenant, God has left nothing out. He says, "You can look ahead and look around. But you can also look within to the righteousness of Christ Jesus."

When you see that a miracle is coming your way, suddenly a trial or test doesn't seem as fierce. Instead of giving in to murmuring, you look at God's Word—and the engrafted Word saves your soul.

But in any trial, never forget that although God has a miracle for the outside, He also has a work that He wants to do on the inside:

"Knowing this, that the trying of your faith worketh patience. But let patience have her perfect work, that ye may be perfect and entire, wanting nothing" (James 1:3,4).

God says, "Not only do I want to bring you a miracle; I also want to build your character."

When you choose to totally rely on the integrity of God's Word and trust Him in a trial, suddenly not only do you get your miracle, but you acquire maturity in your Christian faith. You must be patient, never diverting your eyes from what God has said. **Then** you will be perfect and entire; and **then** you will lack nothing.

Many Christians receive the beginning of the Word, but they don't hold on to it. They let the devil steal that seed. Oh, at first they run around saying, "I've got a miracle on the way!"

But soon their tone changes to, "Dear God, where is it? I've been waiting for five minutes, and my miracle isn't here!"

Eventually, many people lose their vision because they aren't focused on God's Word. They say, "I've waited long enough!" and give up.

James says, "It could be days, months, or even years...but let patience bring forth perfection!"

You see, God doesn't just have something "good" for you; He has something that is **perfect.** But it will only come through patience.

King David had to be patient for 12 years before he received the evidence of his kingship. Samual anointed him while Saul was still Israel's king. And Saul was a miserable, ungodly man. David could have said, "This man is bad news! I'm going to knock him out because I'm supposed to reign as king over Israel."

David could easily have adopted a negative attitude, especially with Saul's open hostility toward him. But that would have been trying to help God. Did you ever notice that God never asked us to help Him? He only asks us to believe Him.

David even had two perfect opportunities to kill Saul, and he still refused to take advantage of them. The first one came when he and all of his loyal followers discovered Saul asleep in a cave:

> *"And the men of David said unto him, Behold the day of which the Lord said unto thee, Behold, I will deliver thine enemy into thine hand, that thou mayest do to him as it shall seem good unto thee. Then David arose, and cut off the skirt of Saul's robe privily"* (I Samuel 24:4).

David's men were all urging him, "Kill Saul! God gave you this big chance."

That shows me something. Even though others may come and say, "God wants you to do this," and "God wants you to do that," you will know whether they are speaking correctly if you've kept your eyes on God's Word. David was well-versed in the Word of God. I'm sure the first thought that came into his mind may have been, "The Law tells me not to kill."

And then he said, "I am not to touch God's anointed. Saul may be a bad king—but he is still God's anointed, so I won't kill him."

Listen to the Word, and listen to your Inner Witness, the Holy Spirit. He wants to lead you into all truth so that you can get your miracle.

I am convinced that David was constantly reading God's Word, especially after seeing that he turned down a second opportunity to kill Saul. He wasn't looking at circumstances. Others may have said, "Two chances! This must be God."

Three or four years had passed by when David discovered Saul asleep on a mountain. He had just as much reason to think, "I've waited long enough," but he didn't kill Saul and get impatient. Instead, he took Saul's sword, and then crossed over to another nearby hill. From there, he shouted, "Saul! Saul! I could have killed you, but I didn't. Here's your sword, if you want to send someone over for it."

Saul was so jealous and hateful toward David. (You talk about "desire, deception, disobedience and death, Saul fit the pattern!) But David made up his mind that he would lack nothing in the end. So when Saul's sin caused his physical death, all of the children of Israel petitioned David in one accord: "Will you be our king?"

David became a king at the people's request. And then God said, "The throne of David will go on forever." Through that eternal throne came our Savior, Jesus Who still reigns today as our Intercessor.

If David had killed Saul and taken the throne by force, his kingly reign would have had limitations imposed on it. But he was patient, and patience bore the fruit of perfection. David came out perfect, entire, and wanting nothing. God said, "He's a man after my own heart."

Don't be impatient. Remember, sin brings death; but God wants to bring you an abundance of life. If you try to take shortcuts, you won't get it. But if you take your test with patience, you'll pass with an A. Don't try to outguess or help God. Just believe Him. When you do, the Bible says you get a special reward:

> *"Blessed is the man that endureth temptation: for when he is tried, he shall receive the crown of life, which the Lord hath promised to them that love him" (James 1:12).*

God says, "What's temptation when I've got a crown of life for you at the end?" He wants you to win; that's why He has a reward for you.

Are you in a trial? I want to encourage you to take these three steps: look ahead—look around—look within. In every place that you look, you will see that the Lord has abundant life for you now—and forever. He says, "Look to Me. I've got better things for you if you'll keep your eyes on Me." What's a test? What's a trial? It's easy to stay free from temptation when you know there is a miracle on the way!

Chapter 4

FREEDOM FROM POVERTY

The difference between tithes, alms, and offerings has been too little recognized by the Body of Christ—and there is a big difference between the three types of giving. Find out the benefits and conditions of each three and walk in newness of financial freedom under the promises in God's Word.

Finances can be such a touchy subject in the Body of Christ. There are those who float around saying, "Believe and receive!" and they never act on the Word even though they quote it to everyone else. Then there are those who murmur and complain because of their financial problems—but they blame it on God: "Oh, God wants me to be poor because it makes me spiritual."

But enough on the two extremes. Those who I am addressing are the Christians who already know that Jesus came to give us life abundantly—in this life on earth. They know the Scripture which David said, "I have never seen the righteous forsaken or his seed begging bread." They know that God desires to meet all of our earthly needs according to His riches in glory. But if the Scripture promises all of these things—why are so many suffering great lack?

Especially in today's economy it is important that God's people be aware of the Bible principles for every part of our life, including finances. This world may be falling apart like a two-dollar watch, but if we are acting on God's Word, we don't need to be influenced by the world's economy.

I get a lot of people saying, "Everyone should invest this way," or "No one should be doing this!" But I don't believe that we have to be moved by the uncertainties of the world's financial system. I know that when we put our finances under God's authority—then we move in the authority of His Word over our circumstances, and we prosper.

A friend of mine says, "If you need love, come to our church; we'll give you God's love." But when I heard that I thought, "If you need love and you're a Christian, you ought to be giving love, because it is in giving that you receive."

The same principle in God's Word applies to three areas of your finances where God is involved: tithes, offerings, and alms.

Each of these three areas are completely different, yet all involve your finances. Each of these areas has specific blessing which apply to them, and so we should make it very important to understand exactly what God says about tithes, offerings, and alms.

This lesson will bring up a forest of results if you do more than just say, "Ho hum; I know the Scriptures about finances." Don't just tune out and say, "I already know all of that." Instead, decide to take God's Word into your Spirit and make it yours. If you've heard it before—don't worry, it's still good for you to hear it again!

The most important part is to take the actions in these Scriptures and start acting on them; and take the promises and begin claiming them. When you combine these two faith principles, you'll see the results. Now look at the first segment of giving: The Tithe:

> *"Bring ye all the tithes into the storehouse...."*
> *(Malachi 3:10a).*

What is the storehouse? That is the place where you receive the Word of God each week. The storehouse is the local church. A lot of people try to say, "Oh, I tithe all over the place; here one week, there the next." But that is not a tithe; that is an offering. There is a big difference, and God wants you to know what it is:

"Bring ye all the tithes into the storehouse, that there may be meat in mine house, and prove me now herewith saith the Lord of hosts, if I will open you the windows of heaven, and pour you out a blessing, that there shall not be room enough to receive it" (Malachi 3:10).

Your tithe makes an open channel through which God can bless you so abundantly that you will have to make more room to receive it. What is that? That is an overflow of blessing. But not only will He bless you; He also promises to halt the work of the enemy against your prosperity, and also bless your nation:

"And I will rebuke the devourer for your sakes, and he shall not destroy the fruits of your ground; neither shall your vine cast her fruit before the time in the field, saith the Lord of hosts. And all nations shall call you blessed: for ye shall be a delightsome land, saith the Lord of hosts,... " (Malachi 3:11,12).

God has designated some very specific blessings and conditions which become yours through faith when you tithe: revelation (meat) in the storehouse is one which many people overlook. People say, "I attend church three times a week, and I'm not getting fed. Boo hoo."

I ask, "Does your church teach the fundamental Word of God?"

Oh, yes."

If that is the case, they should be receiving the meat of God's Word, isn't that right? The Bible says that "to the hungry soul everything is sweet." I believe that if you go to church with an attitude of being hungry for

His Word, just one verse could change your whole day. You say, "I am hungry for God's Word, but I'm not getting meat from it."

That usually happens to Christians who have been eating the Word, eating the Word, and eating the Word—but never giving out what they take in. A person like this is a hearer of God's Word, but not a doer of it. You'll notice that the people who always gripe, "I'm never fed," are the ones who never feed God's Word to others. The problem is that they are spiritually fat.

So if you are lacking in spiritual growth, then start giving out what you already have. Just as exercise makes you hungry, exercising the Word in your life to others will make you hungry for more. Job could say, "I esteem God's Word more than my necessary food," (Job 23:12) because he spent a great deal of his time concentrating on, confessing, and ministering the Word of God.

The number one accelerator to turn spiritual lack into spiritual growth is exercise. I have found that spiritual exercise is simply obedience to the Word of God—and a part of that obedience is through your tithing. God says, "If you tithe, you will have meat in your storehouse."

People say, "I'm tired of milk; I want meat."

Well, the Bible tells you that you get meat from God's Word when you tithe. If you aren't getting it, perhaps you aren't a tither. If you are a tither, perhaps you haven't been expecting and believing that promise! You have a right to the meat of the Word when you tithe. You should come to church saying, "I expect **steak** from God's Word today." I have noticed that God is always faithful to those who come expecting from Him!

But the second thing God promises is where the blessing goes beyond the spiritual and into the physical realm. A lot of people look at the verse that promises a blessing poured out from the windows of heaven, and they say, "That's a spiritual blessing."

No, that is a physical promise. The meat in the storehouse is what is meant to feed your **spirit;** and God is making a distinction between the blessings you will receive. Part is spiritual, and part is physical. This passage of Scripture points out that God isn't simply tossing out a blessing here and there; He is pouring them out on you for being obedient and paying your tithe. As you study the difference between tithes, offerings and alms, you will find that the blessings are very different with each one.

Notice that when the Bible explains the blessings which accompany the tithe, that it isn't speaking of men giving you blessings; it is speaking of blessings coming directly from God. Then to make sure that you enjoy and receive all of His blessings, God says, "I'll rebuke the devourer."

In the New Testament Jesus said, "I gave you authority over the devil." But here is a promise where God says, "That's true, you have authority; but this time I get to rebuke him for you!" That must be a sight to see!

So God has promised both spiritual and physical blessings to those who obediently tithe to Him—and then He promises to rebuke the devourer, so He is saying two things: "he won't pull up the fruit of the spirit out of your life," and "he won't steal the blessings I've poured out on you."

Then God went a step further. He said, "I'm so thrilled about your tithe that I'm even going to bless your whole nation." When the Christians in our nation get involved in local tithing, other nations are going to start wondering why we are so blessed. In fact, I believe that the blessings on our nation today have largely come because Christians were faithful to act literally on God's Word.

The final word from God is that your land will be "delightsome" when you tithe. I looked up the definition of "delightsome," and it means "valuable," "acceptable," or "desirable." Why is the land delightsome? Because God has opened the windows of heaven and poured out His blessing upon it! Because it is a land that is filled and overflowing with the meat of His Word. Tithing will bring God's goodness into places where there was lack; that is His promise to you.

But if you aren't faithful in acting on the Word, you won't get the results it promises. In the same way, if you act on it, you also need to be claiming the promises that go along with it. That is where faith comes in, and faith pleases God.

If you aren't tithing by faith, then start now; you've been cheating yourself out of the blessings that God wants to give you.

People say, "Tithing is Old Testament." That's true. "Tithing is in the Law." That is also true. But Jesus came to fulfill and establish the law—not to abolish it. In fact, tithing not only was a part of the law, but it even preceded the law, because Abraham (the father of faith) was the first tither. He had just won a battle, and then on the way home with the spoil he gave tithes of all he possessed to a priest named Melchizedek. Then in the book of Hebrews God reveals to us that the priest Melchizedek is a "type" of our High Priest, Jesus Christ.

In the Old Testament, when the people brought their tithes, the High Priest would gather them together and offer them in worship to God. So today, Jesus Christ is the One Who receives our tithes, and offers them to Him in worship. Hebrews chapter seven says that our tithes are not paid to earthly ministries, but to our great High Priest, the Lord Jesus Christ.

This is where your tithe requires faith. Stop looking at it as a "local storehouse" situation and realize that your tithe goes far beyond the local church. It goes into heaven itself:

"And here men that die receive tithes; but there he receiveth them, of whom it is witnessed that he liveth" (Hebrew 7:8).

God is saying, "Oh, men may be instrumental in collecting your tithes—but My Son is the One Who receives them."

When you tithe, what is happening? Jesus, your High Priest, receives the tithe, and offers it to God. And the Word tells us that He ever lives to make intercession for us, so I believe He is saying, "Here is the tithe. Now, open the windows of heaven; give them meat in the storehouse; and rebuke the devourer." He intercedes on your behalf, and then God's promise comes to pass in your life.

Jesus, in His earthly ministry, advocated the tithe:

"Woe unto you, scribes and Pharisees,

hypocrites! for ye pay tithe of mint and anise and cummin, and have omitted the weightier matters of the law, judgment, mercy and faith: these ought ye to have done, and not to leave the other undone" (Matthew 23:23).

Jesus was not saying, "As long as you have judgment, mercy and faith, everything is fine."

He was saying, "You need to tithe, but don't forget about the rest!" Jesus had more to say about the importance of the tithe:

". . . then saith he unto them, Render therefore unto Caesar the things which are Caesar's; and unto God the things which are God's" (Matthew 22:21).

The tithe is God's; it is not yours. You don't bring your tithe to church and say, "I'm feeling generous, God, so here is my tithe." That ten percent belonged to Him whether you gave it to Him or not. He is very stern about it in Maclachi 3:8-10.

"Will a man rob God? Yet ye have robbed me. But ye say, Wherein have we robbed thee? In tithes and offerings. Ye are cursed with a curse: for ye have robbed me, even this whole nation" (Malachi 3:8-10).

The tithe has always belonged to God. You think that you have it rough? In the Old Testament they paid not just one tithe, but three of them. They paid the firstfruits of the land, which constituted the first tithe. The second tithe was saved and it provided finances to every family to travel into Jerusalem every year for services.

It has always been important to God that families receive regular spiritual nourishment. The feast days were specifically devoted to giving the Word for hours and hours each day. Then they would go home and teach it to their children. That is why God said, "Talk about it in your home, and when you go out of your home. Talk about My Word in everything that you do, and teach it to your children all the time." This was so important to God that a special tithe was set aside especially to make this teaching possible.

The third tithe came every three years, and it was given to the poor, the widows, and those who needed help. This tithe was given into the temple treasury to be disbursed by the priest as he saw needs in the land.

About each of these required tithes. God said, "They are mine." And when I looked up the Scriptures on tithing I noted that the Bible never says that you "give" tithes. It says that you **pay** tithes.

A tithe is literally "a tenth," and it is paid as "the firstfruit" of your labor. I like to take that literally into my life, and **pay** it to God as my very first bill. Now if I said, "You owe me $10.00," your payment would not be an offering; it would not be a gift. It would be a valid payment, just as God says, "The tithe is a valid payment."

Tithing is paying the money that you owe to God. To withhold it is to rob Him. But then I looked up the word "pay," and it is **shalam,** same word as **shalom,** meaning "peace."

The word means "to be complete," "to be whole," "sound," or "made safe." And God has promised to restore those areas of both spiritual and physical lack through the tithe. You say, "He wants too much."

But God doesn't want your money—He wants **you**. He said, "Where your treasure is, there will your heart be also." You see, through paying your tithe you are opening a door for him to bring soundness into the places of instability. You open the door for Him to make whole what has been lacking, and to make you safe from the devourer. God created the tithe as a benefit to **you**.

People call us on the telephone and a great percentage of them want counseling and prayer for their finances. But I would venture to say that the great percentage of those people have never obeyed God's Word commanding the tithe. You know, often we don't need a lot of financial counsel; we just need to act in obedience to Him, so that He can bless us.

You should expect certain benefits from your tithe. People say, "I'm spiritual. I don't give to receive." Don't worry, then; you won't receive. I think that a lot of supposedly spiritual attitudes have been "religious"—not Scriptural. There is a difference. You say, "Would you pay your tithe if there were no benefits?"

Yes I would, because God commanded it. But interestingly enough, He is so adamant about blessing you through the tithe that He actually challenged us, "Prove Me."

Have you ever proved God? He must want you to expect a blessing if He asked you to prove Him; so when you give, totally obey His Word and expect His promises to come to pass. He gave specific promises with specific action for one reason: to become your source for every need.

It's the same way with offerings. Remember the tithe that was required of the Jews to pay for needs within the church? Those were the equivalent of offerings, an extra tithe which was given above the ten percent. The New Testament mentions that you **give** offerings, you do not "pay" them. You owe tithes, but you offer offerings.

The Bible never says that God will rebuke the devourer, open the windows of heaven, or bless your nation through the offering. People say, "I don't tithe, but I just give offerings." And they are missing some of the wonderful benefits that accompany the tithe. Offerings won't keep the devourer off your back; they won't give you revelation in God's Word. They will not bless your nation. Offerings have their own tremendous benefits, very different from the tithe.

Luke 6:38 uses the word "give," and it tells you the results you can expect through giving offerings:

"Give, and it shall be given unto you; good measure, pressed down, and shaken together, and running over, shall men give unto your bosom. For with the same measure that ye mete withal it shall be measured to you again" (Luke 6:38).

When you give offerings, God does not open the windows of heaven to bless you, but He does move upon the hearts of men to bless you. Offerings are specifically designed with the benefit of moving men to give to you in great abundance. God says, "Men are going to give, give, give, depending on the measure with which you offer."

If you offer generously above your tithe, you will find that God gives you tremendous favor among men. They will give to you without knowing why. Offerings are not paid, and God does not require them of you, and they are not specific amounts. Offerings are given according to your free will, in the amount God moves on your heart to give.

I wondered what the word "give" means, and so looking it up I found that it's definition is "to cast," "to transfer a load or burden," or "to lay a foundation." The last meaning excited me, because essentially an offering is a way to lay a foundation for men to bless you. But let me caution you not to start looking around and saying, "He's rich; he is the one God will use."

People who do that are looking to men as their source, instead of God as their Source. I remember when we had first started our church, we held a prayer meeting for young people every Friday evening at our house. There were nearly forty of them who would come over for this time of prayer and intercession, and God moved beautifully through it—but it absolutely wore out the fabric on our divan and chair in the living room! After an extended period of use, the threads became really worn, and we needed to replace the furniture; but at the same time we couldn't because God moved on my husband and me to give a special offering to help someone else. We simply prayed, "God, this furniture needs replacing," and left it with Him.

It seems as though it was only days after we'd prayed that a woman came to Wally and me after a service to hand us an envelope. She said, "I want to tell you where to put this; and I don't want you to use it for anything else. Don't put it into the ministry, but instead use this money to pay for reupholstering your divan and chair in your home."

We called a man about paying for fabric and labor, and the amount was for exactly what the woman had written her check for! This was a direct result of offering—it was the blessing from men, not from God. Yet while God will use men to bless you, remember that you must look to Him for it.

I have noticed that in any testimony of a person receiving a great blessing from another person, you can trace back and find that they had given offerings to lay a foundation for men to give to them. This is the Scriptural benefit which accompanies offerings.

There is another type of giving which has its own very different benefits and characteristics, and that is alms giving. Of course we as Christians know that we should help the poor; but often we tend to think, "That's a part of my tithe. Let the church give to the poor."

But in Proverbs 19:17 you read, "He that hath pity upon the poor lendeth unto the Lord; and that which he hath given will he pay him again." In the book of Acts you find an account of a cripple begging for alms:

"And a certain man lame from his mother's womb was carried, whom they laid daily at the gate of the temple which is called Beautiful, to ask alms of them that entered into the temple;..." (Acts. 3:2).

Alms are finances which are given over and above your tithe; and they are to help those who are poor. You saw in Proverbs God's promise to repay the money which you give for alms; and you saw that He considers alms to be a loan unto Him. Now 2 Corinthians 9:10 tells us how God pays it back:

"Now he that ministereth seed to the sower both minister bread for your food, and multiply your seed sown, and increase the fruits of your righteousness;... " (2 Corinthians 9:10).

A lot of people tend to think that this passage of Scripture speaks of tithes, but it really is written about alms. This is not ministry to the church; it is ministry to the poor:

"Being enriched in every thing to all bountifulness, which causeth through us thanksgiving to God. For the administration of this service not only supplieth the want of the saints, but is abundant also by many thanksgiving unto God; While by the experiment of this ministration they glorify God for your professed subjection unto the gospel of Christ, and for your liberal distribution unto them, and unto **all** *men;... " (2 Corinthians 9:11-13).*

This money can be given to those believers who are poor, but it can also go to those who are spiritually poor and have not the gospel. Now look at how God pays it back: He multiplies it; it never ends. You see, You are not paying tithes for God to bless you personally, but you are actually sowing seed. You do not pay alms, nor do you give them; you **sow** alms.

When you give to the poor, you could be helping someone who lacks food, shelter or clothing, or you could be giving to missions. But God says, "As you have done it to the least of these, you have done to Me.''

You are lending to the Lord—and He will never be your debtor. You see, always with sowing alms you find a multiplication principle both spiritually and physically. Spiritually, because God says, "I will increase the fruits of your righteousness," and physically because God says, "You will be enriched in all things to all bountifulness. . . ."

If you sow alms to the poor, you are sowing seed; so look at a principle for seed: if you sow lettuce, what happens? You get multiple leaves, not just one leaf. Then, if you keep cutting it back, you get more lettuce. Sowing seeds is always a process of multiplication.

Sowing alms will multiply the work of the fruit of the spirit in your life. If you want more patience, joy, love, or meekness—sow alms and believe for the fruit of the spirit to be multiplied in you. There is something about giving to the poor who do not have their needs met—both spiritually and physically, that works to increase your righteousness.

I see the generous spirit of one who loves to give in a New Testament parable of a man who hired laborers for his vineyard. Whether they came to work for him early in the morning, or in the last hour of the day, each laborer agreed for a penny as wages. But at the day's end, those who had worked longer hours exclaimed, "We should get more than a penny!"

The generous employer said, "No, you all agreed to work for that price. Is your eye evil just because I am good?" He was saying, "You are getting greedy and wanting more, just because I am generous." and the word "evil" really means "stingy."

Some people say "I pay my tithes. I do what's expected," and their giving becomes wrapped up in works without faith. Then when someone has a need, the person says, "Don't ask me. Ask someone with more money," or "Let the church take care of it."

That is shutting out the compassion God wants flowing through you, and you are guilty of having an "evil" eye. Instead of increasing in the fruit of righteousness, you are decreasing it. Proverbs is a book which highlights the divine wisdom of God, and in it Solomon highly exhorted giving. He said, "He that watereth will himself be watered." He said, "The liberal soul shall be made fat." Why? Because sowing alms allows continual growth and multiplication in your spirit and in your finances.

The Bible says that alms will enrich you in every thing to all bountifulness. Then someone comes along and says, "That doesn't mean finances." I'll ask them, "What does every thing mean?" It means "everything," just as it always has! The sowing of alms supplies the want of the poor and the want of the saints because it opens a door for God to bless you in return.

Not only that, but sowing alms brings multiplication of praise and thanksgiving to God. When you sow alms you enrich yourself, increase your righteousness, cause a lot of people to praise God, and increase flows everywhere! It doesn't tell us whether the blessings come from God and men. It can come any possible way.

One of the special places that the increase comes is through bringing forth spiritual children. You see, alms is a way of feeding the Word of God to those who haven't yet heard it. Sowing alms can mean "a field of grain." You can fill them with both spiritual and physical food. That is why in presenting the Gospel, programs of Bible distribution are so vital. Then we provide more than just a gospel message and salvation; we provide a way for new Christians to mature, and grow, and produce the fruit of the spirit—and best of all to bring more souls into the kingdom.

What happens when we share the gospel? We are sowing fields to come up and multiply in the lives of others.

It is exciting to see that God has separate and special promises for every type of giving. God knew that today's economy would be unstable and unpredictable, but He says, "I gave you a way out." In fact, He gave three ways for you to live above the poverty of this world: tithing, offering, and sowing.

How beautifully God has demonstrated that "It is more blessed to give than to receive." For it is through our giving that we "Prove Him." We prove that He is Jehovah Jireh, Who supplies all of our needs according to His riches in glory.

You see, when we Christians will stop murmuring about "what this means," and "what that means," and just start obeying the Word, we're going to have its results. Hebrews 5:14 says, "Strong meat belongs to them...who by reason of use have their senses exercised to discern between good and evil." Strong meat is ready for the Body of Christ, and we'll get it by exercising the principles of God's Word, and a very vital part of that exercise comes through paying tithes, giving offerings, and sowing alms.

God's Word shows us how to live in abundance of

life; it is not a task or a trial. When you obey it totally without a lot of excuses or rationale, that's when you'll see its fullness in your life. I pray that you received this truth into your spirit. You will be fed with the meat of revelation knowledge, see the devourer rebuked, and your nation will be blessed. Men will pour blessing upon you, which you will in turn use to bless others. I know that you will start planting fields of grain to be multiplied in righteousness and spiritual children. Praise God for our marvelous opportunity to live in obedience to His Word!

Chapter 5

FREEDOM FROM INSECURITY

There is such sweet security in knowing the completeness in your position in Christ. Yes, insecurity seems to strike at the most uncomfortable times, and often through the most unlikely situations. But your revelation of the total process of redemption, both sonship and placement through adoption, will free you into the security of who you are.

From the very rich to the very poor, in all segments of society, insecurity is a leveling agent; it is no respecter of persons. As young children perhaps we carried what were called "security blankets." Into circumstances both new and frightening we carried them as warmth of the familiar in strange and unknown surroundings. But we outgrow those security blankets. Some of us outgrew teddy bears, some of us outgrew sucking our thumbs. But all of us know the pangs of insecurity.

God wants to surround you with a security blanket that will free you from the fear of insecurity. He wants you secure in the assurance that He has taken care of each part of your life: past, present and future. I once received a letter from a woman who testified of the security which God filled her life with; and I thought, "Dear Lord, how we all need what this woman has."

She reminded me, "You gave a teaching on David's wife, Bathsheba, and how she was forgiven after committing adultery—and is even in the lineage of Jesus Christ! Her son, Solomon, even said, 'She's a virtuous woman.'"

The woman writing said, "That story relates to me. My unbelieving husband left me and our three young children for another woman. Shortly after, in my hurt and disillusionment, I thought nothing of getting involved with another man—even though I **was** a Christian! I soon found I was pregnant, but he was nowhere around. I didn't want to add the sin of abortion—murder—to my already-existing sin of adultery. I decided to keep the baby."

The woman repented of her sin and promised that she would raise this child according to the admonition of

His Word.

But she said, "After having this new baby I just kept worrying about what to tell my other children. How could I cover up my sin of adultery? I thought the other children would hate me and the baby."

But the Lord showed her, "Your past is over. Your children will not turn against you," He comforted her. She wrote in her letter, "I can now rest peacefully in the security that my children will rise up and call me a blessed, virtuous woman because of the security God has given me in His Word."

She is secure about her past, she is secure about her present, and she is secure about her future. The heartwarming part of her story is the end, for she and her husband were reunited in the Lord and in their marriage. They are a family again and serving Him today. She is a secure woman who found the substance of her security in God's Word. He has a security blanket for every area of your life too, but God's security blankets are only for believers.

Look around. You'll see unbelievers everywhere grabbing every available security they see: money, people, you name it, they're looking for security in it, but outside of God security eludes them. They'll try Eastern philosophy, but it only makes them ask more questions; they have no answers. They'll try drugs or alcohol, but eventually they sober up again. Only Jesus Christ can bring the peace of security because the Bible says, "He IS our Peace." He is our Security.

Jesus Christ has given you security because He made peace between you and God. He gave you something very special: first, He gave you **regeneration,** which is the new birth which makes you God's son. But you are more than a son, for the Bible says you were also **adopted.**

Most Christians know that they have been born again, and they understand that Jesus has given them new life. But few realize that adoption is a separate process. You have been adopted, and that is where your security comes in:

> *"Now I say, That the heir, as long as he is a child, differeth nothing from a servant, though he be lord of all; But is under tutors and governors until the time appointed of the father. Even so we, when we were children, were in bondage under the elements of the world: But when the fulness of the time was come, God sent forth his Son, made of a woman, made under the law, To redeem them that were under the law,..." (Galatians 4:1-5a).*

You were in bondage before you received the precious gift of salvation through Jesus' shed blood. When you were born again you were "redeemed," or purchased back for God's possession. Sin no longer rules as your master, but you now belong to God: you are His child. But you have more than just a title. Galatians 4:5 says that Jesus redeemed us who were under the law for one reason: "...*that we might receive the adoption of sons.*"

You receive the name, "son of God," but it is your adoption by the Father which places you as His son. In the Old Testament when a son was adopted, as Abraham adopted Ishmael, specific customs were observed. You see, although Ishmael's father Abraham was a free man, his mother was a slave. Legally although he was a son, he was still a slave. In order to be a true son he had to be adopted.

We receive the blood of Jesus to become God's sons. But we must also have the adoption which places us in our legal position. Ishmael could only enter into the privileges and authority of a son after being adopted.

After adoption Ishmael receives all the authority that his father has, and he is legally a son. The son is equal to the father. In the same way, the Pharisees were outraged that Jesus called God ''My Father,'' because He was equating Himself with God.

In Paul's generation, Romans practiced adoption of sons. Until age sixteen they were placed under the discipline of tutors. Upon coming of age, the sons celebrated an adoption ceremony which symbolically bestowed the same privileges of his father on him. He was now considered mature enough to handle the responsibility of the position, authority, conditions and blessings of being a son.

When slaves were owned, but there were no children, a master might watch for a slave who would be worthy of becoming his heir. He would look among his slaves and ask himself, ''Who is aggressive? Who is loyal and faithful? I shall adopt that person as my own.''

Sometimes that person was a fully-grown adult, but they were still adopted. Then in the custom the master would say, ''I have chosen to adopt you. You will be my child and carry my name, so from now on you are a son, not a slave.''

Then at the completion of the ceremony the slave who

was now a son would say, "Abba," to his new father; he was saying, "You're my daddy."

As a born again Christian, God is not just some big master who is trying to whip you into shape. He is your daddy, and you are his child. He has adopted you in order to bestow on you every privilege and condition that a son could possess.

My husband and I have an adopted son, so I began comparing natural adoption to supernatural adoption. I thought, "When people adopt children they often choose according to a child's appearance or abilities."

I can tell you what happened to us when we first saw Mike at 3½ years old. We fell in love with him. My husband said, "I can't go home without him."

We adopted Mike spontaneously. We saw him, we wanted him to be our child, and we took him home; it was that simple. We brought him home with us even before the legal work was completed on paper. But your adoption was not spontaneous, for Ephesians 1:4,5 tells you when the Father made plans to adopt you:

"According as he hath chosen us in him before the foundation of the world, that we should be holy and without blame before him in love: Having predestined us unto the adoption of children by Jesus Christ to himself, according to the good pleasure of his will, . . . "

He says, "I wrote your plan of adoption even before the world was created."

You were not predestined to be saved; that was your own choice. But your predestination is found in your adoption. God says, "Everyone who is saved I adopt so they can benefit from the privileges of being in My family."

God predestined your adoption, and it gave him **good pleasure.** He took joy in preplanning for you to be a joint-heir with His Son, Jesus.

Have you ever wondered why God would want more children? After all, He had the best, didn't He? He said about Jesus, "This is my Beloved Son in Whom I am well pleased."

Statistics say that most families who adopt a child will only adopt one. A few will adopt two or three, and a rarer few will even adopt more. But one child is the standard figure on adoption. But God wanted a big family! He didn't just want one or two; for it is His will that not one person would perish, but that He could save every person. Hebrews 2:10 tells us that God wants a big family:

For it became him, for whom are all things, and by whom are all things, in bringing many sons unto glory, to make the captain of their salvation perfect through sufferings."

God wanted to bring many sons into His glory. He desires to bring you into all the privileges that Jesus Christ obtained through His sufferings. Some people say, "Oh, there will be glory when we get to heaven."

But God wants us to have glory now. You are His child, and He wants to be your Daddy while you are living on this earth, and Jesus suffered and shed blood in order to accomplish that work.

When we saw Mike we said, "He is so beautiful and so charming. We want him to be ours."

Most people do adopt by sight. But when God looked at you did He say, "You are a knockout! My, you have a sweet disposition, you would fit right into My family."

Or did He say, "Your IQ is exceptional. I need smart people in My family."

No, God did not choose you according to your looks or IQ. He was not concerned with what you could offer Him. In Ezekiel 16:6 God said that man was polluted with sin. That doesn't sound very enticing.

Ephesians 2:12 says, *"...ye were without Christ, being aliens from the commonwealth of Israel, and strangers from the covenants of promise, having no hope, and without God in the world:..."*

God was looking for some people who were hopeless. He was looking for you:

"Having the understanding darkened, being alienated from the life of God through the ignorance that is in them, because of the blindness of their heart:..." (Ephesians 4:18).

God did not choose you because of your IQ; your understanding was darkened. He didn't get you because you finished college; you were ignorant. He didn't pick you out because of your beautiful eyes; you were blinded to spiritual things. God adopted you because He loved you. He didn't have an adoption list that said, "I only want sweet ones." He said, "I want anyone who will come to me." He wants to be your Daddy. He wants you to know within that He is your loving Father:

"And because ye are sons, God hath sent forth the Spirit of his Son into your hearts, crying,

Abba, Father'' (Galatians 4:6).

It wasn't easy for Him to make you His child. You see, adoption costs money. Today if you adopt a newborn baby typical costs include the mother's hospitalization, legal fees, furniture, clothing, food, and then you keep on paying to bring up the child. A baby is very expensive to adopt. In the same way when the Father adopted you He really had to pay.

You were so dark and polluted with sin that Someone had to die in your place to clean the slate for you. The only One Who would—and could—take your place in death was the very Child Whom God loved the most: His Only Son, Jesus Christ. Jesus Christ was the Son of God, but He came down and became a Son of man. You were a son of man. But through Him you become a son of God. And unlike natural adoption, you even aspire to look just like your Father.

When we adopted Mike, he didn't look like us. Oh, occasionally someone will say, "Mike looks just like you." That really flatters me because to be honest with you, Mike is better looking than all of us. He really doesn't resemble either Wally or me. Now if you look at our natural-born child, Sarah, she looks just like her father; if you've seen Sarah, you've seen Wally. But usually adopted children do not have your behavioral characteristics. And as far as having your behavioral characteristics, they may pick it up along the way but they are not inherited.

But when you get adopted by your heavenly Father it's even better. He makes you look as beautiful as He is:

"But we all, with open face beholding as in a glass the glory of the Lord, are changed into the same image from glory to glory, even as by the Spirit of the Lord" (2 Corinthians 3:18).

The Holy Spirit Who looks just like the Father has come to live inside your spirit. He bears witness that God is your Father. He makes your actions resemble the Father's, and He gives you God's characteristics. Why? Because He cries, "Abba, Father," or "Daddy."

"The Spirit itself beareth witness with our spirit, that we are the children of God:..." (Romans 8:16).

Your heavenly Father has already made the provision to deal with your sinful past. He has destroyed it through the blood of Jesus, and now He has made you His child. You can be very secure about your past because God says, "You aren't a slave to sin any more. You are mine."

Now that He has taken care of your past, He also wants to meet every need in your present life on earth. Your adoption has many benefits for you today. I asked, "Lord, what do we receive through adoption?"

Number one, you receive an inheritance:

"In whom also we have obtained an inheritance, being predestinated according to the purpose of him who worketh all things after the counsel of his own will:...(Ephesians 1:11).

There is that predestination again. God said, "I have not only predestined your adoption; I have also planned ahead for you to receive your inheritance."

We were slaves to sin with nothing coming to us but

hell. In fact, when we were sinners we probably remember having a lot of hell here on earth. We were slaves to Satan. A lot of people say, "I'm just doing my own thing. But they aren't doing their own thing—they're doing Satan's thing, and he is a hard master.

When we were born again and left slavery behind for sonship, we received the inheritance of all that Jesus obtained through suffering and death. He doesn't want you living as a slave. You see, there is a difference between a slave and a servant. A slave has no choice to obey; but a servant of God obeys Him out of love. We serve Him from a motivation of love because He is such a loving Father. He has given us everything that belongs to His firstborn Son:

"Now therefore ye are no more strangers and foreigners, but fellowcitizens with the saints, and of the household of God;..." (Ephesians 2:19).

"And if children, then heirs; heirs of God, and joint-heirs with Christ; if so be that we suffer with him, that we may also be glorified together" (Romans 8:17).

A very special part of your inheritance is that not only were you freed from slavery to sin, you were also freed from the bondage of remembering it. The sin nature enslaved you. People say, "I can't help myself; I just keep failing in life."

Why is that? It is because slaves are in bondage to their masters. But you have been given a new nature in your adoption and inheritance, a nature which brings total liberation:

"For ye have not realized the spirit of bondage again to fear; but ye have received the Spirit of adoption, whereby we cry, Abba, Father" (Romans 8:15).

Now let me ask you a question. How can you be insecure about your present with God as your Daddy? He's such a great Daddy; He granted you freedom for your spirit which in turn frees you from the remembrance of sin.

But if He paid this expensive price for your freedom, why are so many Christians still bound to insecurity? There are many who are secure about one area of their life, but very insecure about something else. I remember having an insecurity about getting married. When I first started to date, and it wasn't until I was sixteen, the young man was almost seven years older than I. My mother was very concerned about it; she said, "He's going to want to get married, and you just started dating. You have college and your whole life ahead of you." Then she told me, "You think that since nobody had dated you before this, that this man might be the last one to come along. But that is not true."

What is fear about not getting married? That is an area of insecurity. Any fear that you get in is a bondage, and insecurity is nothing more than fear. It keeps you from trusting the One Who has everything that you need. But you have the Spirit inside telling you, "Daddy has your provision."

I can tell you from my experience that Daddy brought me the best, and it was at exactly the right time. If God planned for your adoption and inheritance before the foundation of the world, don't you think He has what you need today? As an adopted child of God you have true security.

As you start trusting Him for the privileges of adoption, you can be sure that the world will not understand at all. They're busy worrying about everything: "Aren't you afraid of getting cancer?"

"Did you know that the divorce rates are up?"

"Aren't you afraid about nuclear war?"

The world is bound by a cord of fear and insecurity. As an adopted child of the heavenly Father, your trust is an enigma to all who are spiritually blind:

> *"Behold, what manner of love the Father hath bestowed upon us, that we should be called the sons of God: therefore the world knoweth us not, because it knew him not" (1 John 3:1).*

Christians are really strange ones in the world's eyes. Once a man asked me, "Most women who get in the ministry end up with broken marriages. What makes you think yours will be different?"

I said, "Don't ask what—ask **Who.** The same God Who set me apart for the ministry is well able to make my marriage sweeter every day."

He can do the same for your marriage, too, or for any area of your life. Look to Him. He is more familiar to you than even the best natural father could be. But there is another condition to your inheritance, and it goes along with all of the blessings; that condition is called **chastening.**

> *"For whom the Lord loveth he chasteneth, and scourgeth every son whom he receiveth. If ye endure chastening, God dealeth with you as with*

sons; for what son is he whom the father chasteneth not? But if ye be without chastisement, whereof all are partakers, then are ye bastards, and not sons" (Hebrews 12:6-8).

Discipline is a condition that comes with adoption. If you think you're going to get away with everything, you're not. 1 Peter 2:16 tells us that—we are not to use our liberty for a cloak of maliciousness, but as servants of God. You have been made free from sin, and chastening is a part of staying free of it.

The first time Mike really misbehaved, we had to spank him, and it wasn't easy. Wally cried, and said, "I don't know how I can do this."

But Mike needed the correction, just as you need Daddy's correction. A once-popular theory was that God's correction came through sickness and physical affliction. But would you correct your child in that manner? Of course not! That would be child abuse, and it is illegal; how could we ever imagine that God would discipline us in that manner? If you read Hebrews chapter twelve you discover that the correction of God comes through His Word. In His Word is the discipline for those whom He loves. A loving parent would never let his child do anything he wanted. Would you allow your children to run out in the streets to play just because they want to? "Oh, let him play with the electrical outlets; he's just expressing himself."

You'd better start expressing yourself, or that child is going to get hurt! It's the same way with God. The Father Who created you knows what the best plan is for your life. He wrote the instructions; now it's up to you to read His Word and find out what they are. It's the same way with equipment that we use. If I bought a kitchen appliance, it won't work to full capacity unless I understand the instructions for use. When you willingly come under the authority of your Father's discipline, you will work for Him to your fullest capacity.

Another part of adoption is the forgiveness and cleansing that is included in your inheritance. A natural father might condemn you for something: "You'll never amount to anything. You're a real problem."

But God says, "If you do sin, and you confess it, then I am faithful and just to forgive you."

God will never bring up a past sin that has been forgiven. And because He forgets that sin, He has installed in your new nature the ability to also forget it and leave it alone:

"Let us draw near with a true heart in full assurance of faith, having our hearts sprinkled from an evil conscience, and our bodies washed with pure water" (Hebrews 10:22).

You needed more than an inheritance for your present; you needed a new nature to have the inheritance. You needed more than forgiveness; you needed cleansing inside. Now God says, "I have equipped you with the nature of adoption, so I'm giving you the inheritance that goes with it."

God has given you that inheritance for right now. He wants you to be secure in your present life. He wants you to be able to say, "I'm secure about myself; now I want to minister the same security to others. My needs are met, so I want to meet others' needs."

What good would an inheritance be if you didn't get

it until after you died? Your inheritance is for right now, to take care of your present. But if you are concerned about your future, God's adoption has secured that part of your life also.

You see, when you were adopted you were also given a seal within. In natural adoption after the papers are legally complete, a seal is placed on them saying, "This is official in the eyes of the law."

In the eyes of God, your seal of salvation is official, and it is your promise of eternal life. Just as our son's name became Hickey, your "name" became "Saved," and it is in the Lamb's book of life. Now you have the Spirit inside which will translate you into the glory of your future inheritance: eternal life with your Daddy.

In the future, even your physical body will be restored into the fullness of adoption. You can be secure about your past through repentance; and you can be secure about an inheritance for the present. But you have a promise of redemption for all eternity:

> *"And not only they, but ourselves also, which have the firstfruits of the Spirit, even we ourselves groan within ourselves, waiting for the adoption...the redemption of our body"* *(Romans 8:23).*

You have the promise of physical transformation coming where your body will no longer be under the wear and tear of this world. Jesus has adopted **all** of you, and the restoration leaves you lacking nothing in future results.

1 John 3:2 tells us that although God has given us security for our earthly lives, our future adoption even

surpasses that. It outweighs the advantages of earthly kingship:

"Beloved, now are we the sons of God, and it doth not yet appear what we shall be: but we know that, when he shall appear, we shall be like him; for we shall see him as he is."

You and I, although we receive glimpses in His Word, have no idea of the tremendous fullness of what lies ahead. We will rule and reign with Jesus because of our seal of adoption. And when Jesus appears in glory you will receive the fullness of revelation of Him. You have a glorious transformation ahead.

When we adopted Mike, my husband told him, "A lot of people have children they don't want. Many children aren't planned. Some people want boys, but they get girls. But we looked at a lot of children and babies; we chose you. You are a chosen one."

And today Jesus says to you, "You have not chosen Me; but I have chosen you." You are a chosen one, part of a chosen generation. But even better, you chose Him back. He didn't choose you because you were worth it; He chose you because He loves you.

Now every time you enter into your security by faith, you are really saying, "Abba, Abba."

Every financial or physical miracle in your life is the Spirit crying within you, "God, You are my daddy."

Every restoration in your life is created because you listened to the Spirit of God within you as He whispered, "Daddy."

I pray that you discover how to walk in the security of

the knowledge that God's adoption brings to your past, to your present, and to your future.

Chapter 6

FREEDOM FROM SORROWS

God's Word has quite a bit to say about sorrow. It describes three kinds of sorrow: 1) normal, healthy; 2) bitter, prolonged sadness; and 3) a supernatural, godly sadness that brings great change. Can sadness bring life as well as death? Find out how God wants to free you from wrong, destructive sorrow, and turn your supernatural sorrow into joy!

One of the greatest evidences of your Christianity should be your joy. 1 John 1:4 says that God's Word was given to inspire fullness of joy in you, for every aspect of your life. Even in trials, you can radiate the joy of His presence. Of course life in this world is not easy; Jesus Himself said, "In this world you will have tribulation." But never forget that He also added, "Be of **good cheer,** because I have overcome the world!"

As a Christian who is "alive in Him," you have overcome the world and its hatred, fears, and especially its sorrows.

I have found that sorrow can be one of two things: either very healthy, or very damaging. It can give great release, or it can scar your soul, depending on how you handle it. Three types of sorrow are shown in the Bible: natural sorrow, unnatural sorrow, and (best of all) supernatural sorrow. In your life you will probably encounter all three types—if you haven't already—and God's Word gives both example and exhortation on how you are to deal with them.

Let me point out that just because a crisis may bring sorrow, that does not mean it's wrong to cry. After all, didn't our Lord equip us with our capacity to shed tears? Weeping is not only a natural form of emotional release, it is also very Scriptural:

> *"To every thing there is a season, and a time to every purpose under the heaven: A time to be born, and a time to die; a time to plant, and a time to pluck up that which is planted; A time to weep, and a time to laugh; a time to mourn, and a time to dance;..." (Ecclesiastes 3:1,2,4).*

This passage of Scripture informs you that God has

assigned specific times when weeping is appropriate. He also gave us examples in His Word, in both the Old and New Testaments.

Abraham wept brokenheartedly when his wife Sarah died. Jesus Himself wept over His friend Lazarus and over the stony hearts of His Own people who would reject Him as Messiah. The apostle Paul wept with a great burden for his people, and you can almost feel the sorrow he felt when he wished himself "accursed," if it could save his Jewish people. There is no question that times arise when grief demands weeping.

In particular, most of us connect sorrow with the death of a loved one. You miss them after they die, and of course you mourn over them. This is the first type of sorrow I discovered in the Bible, and it could be appropriately called "natural" sorrow.

NATURAL SORROW

As Christians it is important for us to be cautious in the way we handle grief in our lives. Often death or sickness in a loved one leaves us feeling both helpless and hopeless. But if the person is a born-again believer then the Bible offers you a clear-cut hope:

"But I would not have you to be ignorant, brethren, concerning them which are asleep, that ye sorrow not, even as others which have no hope. For if we believe that Jesus died and rose again, even to them also which sleep in Jesus will God bring with him" (Thessalonians 4:13,14).

You'll be reunited with that loved one in the kingdom of God! So although mourning is natural, remember that you don't sorrow as one without hope. The time comes when you must embrace your hope and set aside the grief.

When my father suddenly died from a heart attack it was a tremendous shock and emotional strain for the whole family. The night of his death, I came home tired, and hurting, and went to bed. But during the night I awakened, bright and alert. At first I thought, "My father didn't really die; that was only a nightmare."

But I could still sense the hurt inside, and I couldn't deny the truth. I knew that his death was as real as the sorrow I felt. As I pondered the previous day's events, something very unusual happened: the angel of the Lord came into my room as a shining light, filled with healing. A feeling of warmth touched my heart and seemed to grow inside, easing the hurt and filling me with hope.

Again the same experience happened to me, and both times it was before my father's funeral. I asked the Lord, "Why did you give me such a wonderful experience with Your angel?"

He said, "Marilyn, I let you enter into a taste of the glory that your father is in right now."

My father's funeral was held just before Christmas. It was based on the theme, "I John, saw the new Jerusalem." (My father's name was John.) I was so profoundly touched when the pastor said, "John is seeing the New Jerusalem this Christmas. That's his Christmas present."

How can you sorrow about that? When a believer dies, you have a great hope. Certainly you miss the person and weep over them; that is the very natural, God-given release of natural sorrow. Yet continued travail and grief distorts the picture, and it is from the devil: I call it "unnatural sorrow."

UNNATURAL SORROW

This is soul-wounding grief, and it usually comes because someone has suffered a severe trauma or loss. Unnatural sorrow does not allow Jesus to heal that area of your soul. Many times, it brings anger toward God. Some people think sorrow will cause you to be a stronger saint. They'll say, "Jesus suffered for me, so I must suffer with sorrow; it's the least that I can do."

I really don't agree. I've seen people with deep sorrow who become bitter—but not better. The Bible never says that God came to give you sorrow. Throughout both the Old and New Testaments you are instead assured and convinced that Jesus came to transform your sorrow into joy:

> "for the Lord hath comforted his people, and will have mercy upon his afflicted" (Isaiah 49:13b).
> "Who comforteth us in all of our tribulation, that we may be able to comfort them which are in any trouble, by the comfort wherewith we ourselves are comforted of God" (2 Corinthians 1:4).
> "The Spirit of the Lord God is upon me; because the Lord hath anointed me to preach good tidings unto the meek; he hath sent me to bind up the broken hearted, to proclaim liberty to the captives, and the opening of the prison to them that are bound; To proclaim the acceptable year of the Lord, and the day of vengeance of our God; to comfort all that mourn;..." (Isaiah 61:1-2).

God does not want you to be immobilized by sorrows; He wants you proclaiming His liberty from them. When you are steadfast in His comfort, you then can share it with others. When your attention is focused on sorrow and yourself, then you aren't in a place where God can use you.

I have found that you can identify people by the things they cry about. If you cry whenever things don't go your way, that should clue you in about an area God wants to deal with. Ask the Holy Spirit to show you any areas of unnatural sorrow in your life. Sometimes looking at those reasons of why we cry may reveal more than we want to know!

One source of unnatural sorrow may be feelings of guilt. I know of a woman who was plagued by guilt after her husband's death, and it was the devil all the way. They had a rocky, stormy, miserable marrige, but after he died she kept thinking, "If only I'd been a better wife. It was my fault."

Parents will suffer the same anguish over a rebellious child, or a child whose life has been stolen. They never let up on themselves: "I should have been a better parent." What happens is they are so harsh with themselves that they can't even hear God's voice!

King David experienced this unnatural sorrow over his son Absalom. Absalom was a beautiful child who grew up to become even more attractive as a young man. The Bible says he didn't have a blemish or flaw from the top of his head to the soles of his feet. His beautiful mane of hair was his pride and joy; it grew so much every year that the length of hair which they would cut off weighed four pounds! When I read that it makes me wonder, "God, why did You waste such hair on a man?"

But Absalom was very aware of his good looks, and he was full of pride and a fiery temper. In fact, the temper drove him to murdering his half-brother Amnon for committing a rape. Then he had to flee in order to save his own life, and he couldn't return home until finally his father David sent for him to reconcile the matter.

Outwardly the relationship between David and Absalom was repaired by their meeting together; but inwardly Absalom was furious. He was probably experiencing rejection because David took so long to make amends; and he was also bitter about David's leniency toward Amnon for committing the rape. Absalom's temper opened the door for a desire to get revenge against his father, and when David was ill, he seized the opportunity. He went into the city and sat by the gate where he seduced the townspeople into favoring him above David:

> *"And Absalom said unto him, See, thy matters are good and right; but there is no man deputed of the king to hear thee. And Absalom said moreover, Oh that I were made judge in the land, that every man which hath any suit or cause might come unto me, and I would do him justice!" (2 Samuel 15:3,4).*

As the townspeople passed by, Absalom would tell them, "My father is too busy for you, but I'm a contemporary who really cares. It's too bad I'm not the king."

He lured the people's loyalty away from David, and

soon a message was sent to his father, "The hearts of the people are after Absalom." Now it was David who had to flee, but if that wasn't enough, Absalom was pursuing him to take his life.

But instead of Absalom having David killed, David's men killed Absalom, even though he had instructed them to spare his life. You would imagine what David could have told his men, "Kill him! He's been a troublemaker all his life!"

But instead he said, "Spare him." In spite of his request his men killed his son anyway. Why? Because Absalom defied God's Word, and God did not want him to reign as king.

You say, "David wasn't exactly perfect; he committed murder and adultery." But David was also a repenter. God commissioned him to be Israel's king until his death. He was so softhearted that he even loved Absalom after all of that trouble.

How deeply I am touched by his sorrow every time I read the words he cried out when they sent word that his son was killed:

"And the king was much moved, and went up to the chamber over the gate, and wept: and as he went, thus he said, O my son Absalom, my son, my son Absalom! would God I had died for thee, O Absalom, my son, my son!" (2 Samuel 18:33).

I still think, "David, Absalom only wanted to be a big chief! He didn't care about anyone but himself. He stole your throne and tried to have you killed, and you're wanting to die for him?"

Instead of feeling victorious about placing David

back on the throne, the people were really ashamed and embarrassed. They all went into mourning with David and began to hang back. Thank God that Joab, his nephew and military leader, didn't follow the crowd. He became bold with David:

"In that thou lovest thine enemies and hatest thy friends. For thou hast declared this day, that thou regardest neither princes nor servants: for this day I perceive that if Absalom had lived, and we all had died this day, then it had passed thee well" (2 Samuel 19:6).

Wow, that really jerked David back into the real world! Joab told him, "We came against your enemies, we won the throne back for you, and you're just whining around about Absalom's death. You act as though you hate your friends and love your enemies! Get with it!"

Sometimes just one strong, blunt person will pull you out of unnatural sorrow. After my father's death I watched mother slip into terrible grief that just seemed to hang over her. Finally I asked her, "Did Jesus carry your sins for you?"

"You know that He did."

"Did He carry your sicknesses?"

"Yes."

"What about your sorrows?"

"Yes," she said, "He carried them."

"Then are you going to keep carrying them, or let Him carry them?" After that, it was as though she realized that Jesus wanted to heal that hurt area. You see, you can choose to stay in natural sorrow, but then you can cross over into unnatural sorrow. David was going through unnatural grief over Absalom, and I believe it was inspired by guilt. He may have wished he'd trained him more. He may have thought, "I could have been a better parent."

Guilt will make the burden of sorrow so much more difficult to bear. Certainly David could have done better, but who couldn't? Is anyone a perfect parent? If you are wrong then repent, but let God release you from the sorrow; don't let the devil drag you further into it.

I saw a picture of unnatural sorrow in the book of Ecclesiastes:

"I have seen servants upon horses, and princes walking as servants upon the earth" (Ecclesiastes 10:7).

This is an unnatural situation because servants are supposed to walk and princes are supposed to ride. The Lord created our spirits to be princes which rule over our soul and emotions—even over sorrows. But the devil tempts us to let our souls or our flesh get up on the horse. As long as your spirit is not on the horse, you will not have dominion. God says, "That is unnatural! Get your spirit back in control."

When your soul rides the horse, unnatural sorrow seems impossible to conquer. But when you get your spirit back up on the horse by receiving the comfort God has for you, then you will be in dominion over it. If you have been choosing to stay in unnatural sorrow over a situation then repent! And that is the third type of sorrow.

SUPERNATURAL SORROW

"For godly sorrow worketh repentance to

salvation not to be repented of: but the sorrow of the world worketh death" (2 Corinthians 7:10).

Repentance is godly sorrow and it means that you turn from your flesh and soul, toward God. You get your spirit in control so that area of your life won't bring you down again. And it isn't always easy.

Most of the time we have no problem in dealing with someone else about the sin in their life. But when it comes to God dealing with you specifically, you may find it hard to face up to. I always say that you need to run TO God, not FROM Him. When He is correcting you for something you actually have four alternatives. First of all, you can **deny it.** You could simply pretend that you don't recognize God's voice—although you do. But when you deny God's dealing in your life then you have to pretend, and that burdens your soul. You can say, "I'm not doing anything at all; that's not a sin," and act as sweet and innocent as a little lamb. You can shrug off the blame: "It's everyone else's fault but mine." But deep inside you know that won't cut it with God, and it will not change your situation.

Your second alternative is to try to **change yourself.** You say, "I'll never do that again. Never!"

And what happens? You end up relying on your own strength to change something that only God can change. You sin again. You fall into the trap again, and you're sorrowful over it. Finally you give up and say, "I can't change."

Choice three in how to deal with conviction is to simply **admit the sin,** and stop there. You say, "That's right. I'm a sinner and I feel terrible about it."

But the only affect that admitting your need will have is that you will work yourself into regret and remorse. Exactly what happened with Judas. Oh, he felt so badly about betraying Jesus. He was filled with regret and desperation. But he did not repent.

I have found that people who won't let conviction work its way into their hearts are the ones who are suicidal, as Judas was. If only he had gone the final step into repentance he could have changed his entire situation.

Repentance is your fourth alternative. When Godly sorrow comes, repent! The prodigal son repented after he took his inheritance and really ended up in a mess after spending it all. He spent every dime and ended up feeding pigs. Then he reasoned, "Even my father's servants get more than I. The pigs even eat more! I'm starving."

Then he went out to beg, and I'm sure that was the effect of regret; he tried to fix things himself. But finally he said, "I have sinned, father, against heaven and against you."

Repentance is the only real alternative. No other "option" will bring you back into a place of favor with God. When the prodigal son poured out his heart in repentance his father held out his arms: "You won't be my servant, you will be my son."

The son received back all that he had lost—and more. Supernatural sorrow is so good for you. It turns you back in the right direction where you can again receive your heavenly Father's love and blessings.

Unfortunately I've run across people who refuse to

touch the subject of sin. They'll tell you, "Just walk by faith," and somehow they forget that it still takes faith to repent. It demands faith on your part to believe God's forgiveness and allow Him to bring you out of that sin. John the Baptist's message shocked the Pharisees because they couldn't believe that repentance could come as simply as by faith.

When Paul corrected the Corinthian church he said, "I rejoiced not that you were made sorry, but that you sorrowed to repentance."

We aren't to stay in regret or remorse; we are supposed to identify the sin and move on to repentance:

"And lest, when I come again, my God will humble me among you, and that I shall bewail many which have sinned already, and have not repented of the uncleanness and fornication and lasciviousness which they have committed" (2 Corinthians 12:21).

He is saying, "Listen, you had better straighten things out before I come. If you don't, I'm going to start calling the shots when I get there."

In other words: "Repent!" Even Jesus' final message to the church in Revelation was "Repent!" John the Baptist introduced the Messiah by saying "Repent!" God knows that repentance is very good for us.

I saw the whole pattern of denial and remorse in the life of Saul. He did everything but repent, and his life is an example of what to watch out for. Saul was Israel's first king, and God anointed him to rule. Everything seemed to run smoothly until one day when he got involved with sin and disobedience—intentionally.

He was instructed to await Samuel the priest, arrival; but time for battle was near, and the required sacrifice had not been made. In his impatience, Saul made the obligatory sacrifice himself. He knew that only priests were supposed to perform sacrifices—never kings.

Then when Saul went into later battle with a group of Amalekites, he disobeyed again. God said, "Kill all of them; kill all of their animals; and don't spare their king, Agag."

But instead of following God's command, Saul spared the finest cattle, and neither did he kill Agag.

Samuel caught Saul red-handed in his disobedience, and yet look at Saul's first words upon seeing Samuel approach him: *"Blessed be thou of the Lord: I have performed the commandment of the Lord"* (1 Samuel 15:13).

Samuel thought: "You big liar, you didn't do it at all." This is step one: covering the sin; pretending it isn't there. You can put up a smokescreen and say, "What are you talking about? That's a sin?" But you know you aren't hiding from God. God knew what Saul had done, and so did Samuel:

"And Samuel said, What meaneth this bleating of the sheep in mine ears, and the lowing of the oxen which I hear? And Saul said, They have brought them from the Amalekites: for the people spared the best of the sheep and of the oxen, to sacrifice unto the Lord thy God; and the rest we have utterly destroyed" (1 Samuel 15:14,15).

Here Samuel gave Saul an opportunity to repent; that is God's mercy because He wanted Saul to be the king. But now Saul's lying slants into an even worse direction: blaming someone else. "It was the people's fault."

But hiding your sin will never bring you into the place where God can bless. I hear those types of cop-outs all the time: "If the ushers weren't so mean I'd go to church."

"If there weren't so many hypocrites I'd get right with God."

Placing the blame will not get you anywhere. That's nothing but a big cop-out, and you are running from the voice of God. You know, it takes more strength to play "charades" than it does to just confess the sin, repent, and receive God's forgiveness and cleansing. Saul could have repented and moved into God's blessing, but he **refused,** in spite of direct confrontation from Samuel.

"Wherefore then didst thou not obey the voice of the Lord, but didst fly upon the spoil, and didst evil in the sight of the Lord?" (I Samuel 15:19).

That is direct! Samuel said, "Saul, YOU did it; YOU are guilty. I know of your sin; you know of your sin, so stop lying. Repent!"

What was Samuel trying to do? Change Saul's hardness of heart by showing him the seriousness of the situation. He wanted Saul to obey God. But it just seems that Saul kept getting deeper into his lies:

". . . Yea I have obeyed the voice of the Lord, and have gone the way which the Lord sent me, and have brought Agag the king of Amalek, and

have utterly destroyed the Amalekites" (1 Samuel 15:20).

What is he doing? Pretending he wasn't aware that Agag was to be killed: "That's a sin?" He is still covering his sin:

"But the people took of the spoil, sheep and oxen, the chief of the things which should have been utterly destroyed, to sacrifice unto the Lord thy God in Gilgal" (1 Samuel 15:21).

He still blames the people! I thought, "Saul, it would have been better if you kept your mouth shut. All these lies!" Have you ever noticed that it never stops with just one lie? That's how the devil operates. Finally Samuel just had to lay it on the line:

"And Samuel said, Hath the Lord as great delight in burnt offerings and sacrifices as in obeying the voice of the Lord? Behold, to obey is better than sacrifice, and to hearken than the fat of rams" (1 Samuel 15:22).

People run around doing wonderful deeds saying, "Oh, I may sin occasionally, but I mean well." Or, "I do a lot of good things for God."

God doesn't want sacrifice. In fact, when you give Him your obedience first, then the sacrifice comes naturally; it's not a sacrifice to you, but it comes from your heart.

Samuel said, "Your rebellion is just as bad as outright witchcraft." And Saul's life ended with him consulting a witch for guidance: one is as bad as another. Oh, he was full of remorse when he lost God's counsel, but he would never repent.

How merciful God is! Samuel kept dealing with Saul, and finally Saul tried to compromise his way out:

"...I have sinned: for I have transgressed the commandment of the Lord, and thy words: because I feared the people and obeyed their voice. Now therefore I pray thee, pardon my sin, and turn again with me, that I may worship the Lord...yet honour me now, I pray thee, before the elders of my people, and before Israel, and turn again with me, that I may worship the Lord thy God" (I Samuel 15:24,30).

Dear God, he's still worried about what the people think! He says, "This small episode can be our secret Samuel. The people don't need to know; let's pretend it never happened."

True repentance says, "I don't care what people think; it's me and God, and no one else."

God didn't want to take Saul's kingdom; He gave him several chances to repent with direct dealing through Samuel. But Saul's disobedience hardened his heart against godly sorrow for repentance. He let it stop at regret, and it never went any further. Regret will damage your relationship with God.

God said, "Saul, I am giving your kingdom to another." From that time on, Saul lost dominion over the nation of Israel. Later when David killed Goliath, God gave him favor. The people of Israel sang, "Saul has killed his thousands—but David has killed his tenthousands!"

David was anointed to be Saul's successor, and he committed a few big sins, like Saul. He never consulted a witch for counsel, but he got involved in some things that Saul never did.

David got involved in adultery with Bathsheba, and then he just kept on trying to figure out how he could hide it—especially after he found out that she was expecting a child! He tried to bring the woman's husband home from battle and convince him to go to Bathsheba: "That way, he'll think the child is theirs."

When Uriah said, "No, I can't see my wife, I'm supposed to be in battle." David was really stuck. The only solution seemed to be, "Kill Uriah!" He sent a message to his military leader and said, "Put him in the front lines; make sure he gets killed." Now he was not only an adulterer, but a murderer too. You see, the devil never stops with one sin. There is no such thing as "one small sin." He wants to get you in so deep that it seems hopeless to escape.

God sent a man named Nathan to David, just as He had sent Samuel to deal with Saul. Nathan told David about his sin through a parable:

"There were two men in one city; the one rich, and the other poor. The rich man had exceeding many flocks and herds: But the poor man had nothing, save one little ewe lamb, which he had bought and nourished up: and it grew up together with him, and with his children; it did eat of his own meat, and drank of his own cup, and lay in his bosom, and was unto him as a daughter. And there came a traveller unto the rich man, and he spared to take of his own flock and of his own herd, to dress for the wayfaring man that was come unto him: but took the poor

man's lamb, and dressed for the man that was come to him" (2 Samuel 12:1a-4).

Nathan said, "This rich man had everything, but it wasn't enough. He had to take the most precious possession from the poor man, even though it was all he had."

When David heard that it grieved his soul. He was furious. He said, "The man that hath done this thing shall surely die: And he shall restore the lamb fourfold, because he did this thing, and because he had no pity."

And as soon as David set out judgment, Nathan looked him in the eye and he said, "You're the man. You had everything, and you stole all that Uriah had—even his life."

When Nathan said, "You're the guilty one," David didn't try to hide any more. He didn't say, "I'm the king! Have his head cut off!" He said, "Yes, I'm guilty."

He didn't try to excuse his sin. He didn't try to blame it on someone else. He said, "It's me." Godly sorrow led David into repentance, and later David could say, "You are the God of those who repent."

How do we repent? The Bible tells us how: "If we confess our sins, then he is faithful and just to forgive us, and to cleanse us from all unrighteousness" (1 John 1:9).

You must confess your sin, and the word "confess" means "to say the same thing to God."

David was agreeing with God, "Yes, I am a sinner, and I need Your forgiveness and cleansing." Psalm 51 is the repentance and godly sorrow that he poured out in words with the conviction of his heart:

"Have mercy upon me, O God, according to thy lovingkindness: according unto the multitude of thy tender mercies blot out my transgressions. Wash me thoroughly from mine iniquity, and cleanse me from my sin. For I acknowledge my transgressions: and my sin is ever before me. Against thee, thee only, have I sinned, and done this evil in thy sight: that thou mightest be justified when thou speakest, and be clear when thou judgest" (Psalm 51:1-4).

Did He get free? Yes, he did. David said, "Wash me from my sin and cleanse me from it." Because he agreed with God by saying, "I need Your mercy," he was now in a position to receive perfect forgiveness.

But David goes even further. Because sometimes after repentance we need to ask God to touch and fill those empty areas that He has cleansed. Nowhere else in the Bible do I find a more beautiful example of this:

"Create in me a clean heart, O God; and renew a right spirit within me. Cast me not away from thy presence; and take not thy holy spirit from me. Restore unto me the joy of thy salvation; and uphold me with thy free spirit" (Psalm 51:10-12).

Then at the Psalm's end, David says:

"The sacrifices of God are a broken spirit... Then shalt thou be pleased with the sacrifices of righteousness, with burnt offering and whole burnt offering: then shall they offer bullocks upon thine altar" (Psalm 51:17a,19).

In God's eyes, repentance is the ultimate sacrifice.

When it comes right down to His Word, He isn't interested in your sacrifice—He wants **you.** He wants the sacrifice of your self unto Him. That is repentance. Unless we allow His godly sorrow to bring cleansing and change to our hearts, we tend to take the harshness of our remorse and heap it on others.

Again, I saw this in Saul's life. He wouldn't deal with his own sin. But when his own son Jonathan made a knicky-knacky mistake, Saul was right on him. When the Israelites were to go into battle, Saul issued a command to fast: "Nobody eat today!"

But then Jonathan ate a small taste of honey, and his single action got everyone else started. Saul found out about it. "Who started this?" he demanded, and when he discovered that Jonathan was the offender, he passed his judgment: "Kill him."

How harsh Saul was toward Jonathan, his son; and yet how soft on himself. The condemnation he tried to push down, subconsciously came out toward others. You see, unless we are walking in the cleansing that comes through repentance, we are not walking in love.

In contrast, David was hard on himself, but easy on Absalom. What happens in situations of deep grief? That is when Jesus wants to come in with His promise of comfort:

"Blessed be God, even the Father of our Lord
Jesus Christ, the Father of mercies, and the god
of all comfort" (2 Corinthians 1:3).

You say, "I don't feel close to God, even after I repent." Then read what His Word has to say about His love toward you. But even more, you have another comfort:

> *"And I will pray the Father and he shall give you another Comforter, that he may abide with you for ever;..." (John 14:16).*

In His love and concern toward you, God has offered two kinds of comfort: **objective** and **subjective.** The Scriptures comfort you objectively as you read them; but the Holy Spirit within you wants to work with the Word to help soothe those pangs. God does not want you unnecessarily grieving; He wants to be your comfort: on the outside, and on the inside. It's that important to Him.

There is one more type of sorrow that is also very supernatural. It is not the sorrow of repentance, but it is described beautifully in Psalm 30:5:

> *"For his anger endureth but a moment; in his favour is life: weeping may endure for a night, but joy cometh in the morning" (Psalm 30:5).*

What kind of weeping is this which brings joy in the morning? These are the tears of intercession. This is the burden of bearing God's sorrow over unsaved souls, and unrepented sin in the world. When you bear the burdens of others through intercessory prayer before God, He is watching. Such tears are very precious to Him.

Psalms 126:5 promises that *"They who sow in tears will reap in joy."* There are persecutions with God's calling, and sometimes there are intercessions that seem unending. But did you know that your tears are an investment for future joy? If you have been weeping over a lost or persecuted brother or sister, your joy is on the way.

Revelation 21:4 says, *"And God shall wipe away all tears from their eyes; and there shall be no more death, neither sorrow, nor crying, neither shall there be any more pain: for the former things are passed away."*

You know that joy is on the way in this life; but God also promises a day when you will no longer sow in tears. Meanwhile, no tear of intercession ever goes unnoticed by God. Psalm 56:8 says, *"Thou tellest my wanderings: put thou my tears in thy bottle: are they not in thy book?"*

God wants to heal you from the pain of natural sorrow; and He wants to deliver you from the agony of unnatural sorrow. He wants to cleanse your heart through repentance. And He watches over your intercessory sorrow: that is seed that says you have been interceding for His burden: souls which must be saved.

You could go out and have a pity-party, but I don't think that God cares much for those tears. He wants to bring you out of pity and into the realm of faith. But when you start crying faith tears over the lost, honey, He's writing it down. You're going to reap from those tears!

Chapter 7

FREEDOM FROM WRONG EATING HABITS

We all eat, don't we? Some of us overeat, some of us undereat, and some of us are total buffs about nutrition. Recognizing this fact, I knew that whatever category you fall into, we still have a responsibility to understand what God has to say about food in our lives...and He has a lot to say about it!

Did you know that God outlined a plan for your health in His Word? The Scriptures are so practical and helpful that God hasn't neglected one aspect of our lives. His Word isn't some pie-in-the-sky fantasy; rather, it is a book you can live by because it works.

Somehow when I teach about eating habits, the room I am teaching in seems to get more quiet than usual. I think that a lot of us get so busy with spiritualizing God's Word that we forget to bring it into "where we live." But God hasn't forgotten to do that. He has given many guidelines to cultivating right food patterns—and being set free from wrong ones.

Wrong eating habits are nothing new; in fact, what was the first thing to get Adam and Eve in trouble? It was eating the forbidden fruit. Then there was Esau who sold his own birthright to his younger brother, Jacob, for lentil soup. His lust for food brought him trouble for the rest of his life because he lost the blessing that was rightfully his.

Nebuchadnezzar's grandson, Belshazzar, lost his Babylonian kingdom to Persian rule one night during a feast where he defiled holy vessels by drinking from them, using them to worship false gods.

Another man who was a priest actually died from being far too overweight. Eli was fatter than a forty-pound robin, according to the book of Samuel, and his tremendous desire for food was also picked up by his own sons. They acquired a taste for the fatty meat which was sacrificed, and soon Eli's sons were stealing it from the sacrifices to eat themselves.

Finally God said, "Eli, you either control those boys, or lose your ministry. I'm giving you a choice."

God cautioned Eli twice, but he chose to ignore the warnings. His lust for food and neglect of discipline (on himself and his sons) brought judgment. God said, "You esteem your sons more than you esteem Me."

This is so sad because Eli really did love God; but he had too many indulgences that distracted him from wholehearted service. In the end, His sons were slaughtered in battle, and in that battle the ark of the covenant was siezed. Upon hearing the news, the Bible tells us that Eli fell backward. I believe that he had a heart attack due to his overweight condition.

The point is that eating is a major "idol" of today, even in churches. A lot of people say, "I don't sin," but to them going to church is their big opportunity to go out and eat with friends. Eating is not wrong. But when it comes as a priority before God, eating can bring big trouble.

We tend to forget that the word "lust" can be associated with more than just money or sex; it can also be associated with food, and many Christians fall into it. I don't just want to say, "It's bad to have a lust for food," but I want you to understand how the snare comes along. I found that God has already told us how the snare comes, and I've experienced it in my own life.

I discovered the trap one day when I began wondering about why I would occasionally get hit with an extreme craving for Hershey bars. Thank God it doesn't happen often, but when I get the craving it's hard to resist. When I started analyzing the times that I really craved Hershey's with almonds, I found that the "temptations" arose at specific times of low activity.

"Slothfulness casteth into a deep sleep; and an idle soul shall suffer hunger" (Proverbs 19:15).

Did you know that you are more prone to hunger pangs during inactive times than active ones? Have you ever noticed that when your mind isn't centered on any specific activity, it is too easy to run by the refrigerator every five minutes? An idle mind is attracted to food like a magnet. When you are in a slothful frame of mind, you are a prime target for food cravings, preoccupations—and eventually obsessions.

I thought about how cravings seem to hit whenever I am really relaxing. I'm not against relaxation, but this is sheer idleness, and we all have those types of times. Idleness of the soul—mind and emotions—can bring hunger pangs when you aren't hungry at all. Think about Thanksgiving or Christmas day. Usually you snack first, then eat a big meal, and then snack for the rest of the day. Then in the evening you eat dinner again. Why? Because you are hungry? No, but because of idleness.

According to Proverbs 13:25, this type of gorging is not conducive to satisfaction; instead, the more food you eat, the more you desire:

"The righteous eateth to the satisfying of his soul: but the belly of the wicked shall want" (Proverbs 13:25).

You can eat until you think, "That was good," and are satisfied. But you can also step beyond that pattern and stuff yourself until discomfort settles in. Oh, God wants you to **satisfied** with your meals, but He does not recommend that you step past the boundaries of satisfaction. Have you ever noticed that at times the food tastes so delicious that you just keep eating? That is a trap of lust for food, and God says, "The righteous are not to eat beyond satisfaction."

Many times overeating occurs because you think, "Maybe I won't get this food next week."

This begins a vicious cycle because soon food has you, instead of you having it. I saw this principle in Proverbs 27:7:

"The full soul loatheth an honeycomb; but to the hungry soul ever bitter thing is sweet" (Proverbs 27:7).

What is a full soul? This is a soul that is occupied with God's Word. Your soul is your mind and emotions which are full and complete, meaning "not easily distracted." But the hungry soul, the man whose mind and emotions are undisciplined by God's Word, is preoccupied by food constantly. He craves food and doesn't care what it is, so even bitter food tastes sweet.

After seeing these principles: slothfulness, eating beyond satisfaction, and a dissatisfied soul, I knew that God was saying that our activity and focus was very important in controlling the lust for food. God wants to help us discipline our souls to the control of our eating habits.

I remember having traveled to Finland with a group of pastors and seeing that every other shop sold pastries. Who doesn't like baked sweets? They're marvelous; but after trying every different kind among ourselves, we found out why the Word refers to them as "deceitful dainties." Although they may seem to fill your stomach, they aren't good for you, and you're hungry again an hour after eating them.

"Be not desirous of his dainties: for they are deceitful meat" (Proverbs 23:3).

Overindulgence—and sometimes I think indulgence at all—in sweets is now being recognized as extremely harmful to the body. Yet Solomon recognized that fact in his day, long before nutritionists were popular. You say, "I'll just eat honey, then."

But in Old Testament times even too much honey was to be frowned upon. As in all things the balance of temperance is the key. Proverbs 25:27 warns us that it isn't good to eat much honey; I believe the warning comes because God knew that preferences for sweets were nurtured through—again—overindulgence in them.

On the other side of the scale, some people overindulge in salty food; and with others it is high-cholesterol food such as fatty meat (Remember Eli?) We used to prescribe steak for anyone who was suffering from chronic exhaustion, feeling sure that they lacked the protein that it would supply.

Then came the day when authorities on nutrition began finding that there had been an overemphasis on meat, especially those meats such as pork or beef. People whose diets consisted of too much of these foods were now suffering from circulatory problems brought on by excess cholesterol which had accumulated in their system. The Bible states that any food to excess is wrong:

"Be not among winebibbers; among riotous eaters of flesh" (Proverbs 23:20).

A diet too heavily laden with meat is equally as unhealthy as a diet of too many sweets. God is saying "Balance is the key."

I heard that the average American's diet consists of only fifteen basic foods, while there are hundreds of varieties of **beans alone** in the United States! When God provided us with such great variety, we should use His wisdom and put it to use. By ignoring what He has given us, we often cheat our bodies of the necessary vitamins and nutrients; again the word is **balance.**

You say, "I have too many poor eating habits." Certainly you aren't alone! It's nothing new: Adam, Esau, Belshazzar, Eli and his sons all got into trouble over food, and it is no different with millions of people today. Eating is a national pastime, so how can we turn our eating habits around?

My first suggestion is to have the desire to change poor eating habits. Whether your downfall is overeating, or simply overemphasis, either or both can constitute food lusts. But if you desire to do **all** things as unto God, then you will want to change your eating patterns to glorify Him. You will desire to start eating a healthy variety of foods to bring health to your body—the temple of God.

But as you take action, let faith do some of the legwork too. I know that faith accelerates tremendous restoration of health. Certainly we should also confess the Word over our health and eating habits. But I think it is wrong to confess the Word and then not line up in your actions. What if someone said, "I've got so much faith that I threw away my toothbrush!" I'd say, "That isn't faith; it's bad breath and tooth decay."

Our actions should line up with God's Word to enhance right eating patterns. If you have had a problem lusting over wrong foods or excesses of food, then food is playing the wrong role in your life. God has practical answers for you, starting in 1 Corinthians 10:31.

"Whether therefore ye eat, or drink, or whatsoever ye do, do all to glory of God" (1 Corinthians 10:31).

If we Christians would let this Scripture be a measure against all of our actions we would be free from excesses. I have found that it is an excellent Scripture for balancing out those stray eating habits and bringing them in subjection to Christ. Do all to the glory of God! When you eat ask yourself, "Does this bring glory to God?" Does overeating bring Him glory? Does your appearance bring Him glory?

I am not placing an overemphasis on our appearance; but I am saying that God wants to be a part of every aspect of your daily life, including your eating habits. He wants to be glorified in your body, as well as your soul and spirit.

Proverbs 23:2 has a really heavy Scripture which says, *"And put a knife to thy throat, if thou be a man given to appetite."*

I am not saying that you should cut your throat, but I **am** saying that Christ wants to crucify the bondages of wrong eating patterns. He said, "I know that habit is hard for you. But take it to the cross and reckon yourself dead to it, and I'll deliver you from it."

Don't worry. You won't starve, although I'm sure

that crucifixion of excessive appetite makes it sound as though you will. If you are attacked by hunger pains or you are wrestling with and dreading them, then I have a Scripture for you that I claim all the time. It is Proverbs 10:3:

> *"The Lord will not suffer the soul of the righteous to famish; but he casteth away the substance of the wicked"* (Proverbs 10:3).

I have actually known people to use this Scripture in the fight of faith against desire to overeat—especially when they face the uncomfortable reminder of hunger pangs. It is especially effective for myself and many others.

But I am convinced that Romans 8:26 has revealed one of the best possible keys for doing away with bad eating habits:

> *"Likewise the Spirit also helpeth our infirmities:..."*

An infirmity is a weak area, or a place where the work of the Spirit has not been produced in your life. If you have a weakness in the area of your eating habits, pray in the Spirit before your meal; pray in the Spirit before you open the refrigerator. I'd suggest reinforcing that weak area by setting aside ten minutes of praying in the Spirit before any meal, and you'll find that you eat less; you crave healthy foods. In fact, if you'll just pray in the Spirit as a rule before you open the refrigerator, you'll never devour another whole blueberry pie **either!**

An unruly appetite will become a spirit-dominated appetite if you will remember these tips: keep your mind busy and keep your life active; do everything to the glory of God; crucify your appetite by reckoning yourself dead to it; speak the Word of God over your eating; and pray in the Spirit.

It seems as though some people expect me to prescribe fasting as an agent against wrong eating habits, but too often it becomes an excuse for breaking the fast with a whole pizza pie. It can be a way to keep your flesh in subjection to your spirit, but I do not recommend it as a diet-aid because, really, that is not why we fast. We fast to set aside special time for God, not to lose weight. Really, if you just take the time to let Him dominate and correct your eating habits you will find that you lose weight without having to go through life thinking about food all the time. Most people who want to diet are so busy thinking about what not to eat, that they end up eating more than ever. The Holy Spirit-controlled life is the best way to curb wrong habits.

Now let's see what kind of reinforcement the Bible uses to encourage right ways to eat. Proverbs 18:20 is an excellent place to start:

"A man's belly shall be satisfied with the fruit of his mouth; and with the increase of his lips shall he be filled" (Proverbs 18:20).

In other words, you're going to get what you speak aloud. If you walk around saying, "I'm starving, I eat too much," or statements in the same negative frame, you're courting failure. But if you start speaking words of faith over your appetite, and over your healthful diet, you will discover that you are satisfied with right foods.

As our children grew up they learned to abide by a rule which encouraged them to eat nutritionally wise food: nobody ever came to the table and said, "I hate that food.''

Every person present was expected to take **something** of each food on his plate and eat it whether they liked it or not. What happened? They began liking every food. When my son was twenty he expressed his disgust toward the idea of grown people being picky eaters. He said, ''I like everything.''

Why did he like everything? It was because we spoke right words about the food and acted on them. When we ate meals together my husband would say, ''We like everything here. We like it all.''

Speak right things before you eat: ''I'm satisfied with this food; I do not overeat, but I enjoy what I eat.''

Faith should be a working element in every area of your life, and it can change your eating habits.

A man's belly shall be satisfied with the fruit of his mouth. But even more, you can be satisfied with crackers and milk, if that's all that is available to eat. Proverbs 15:15 says, *''All the days of the afflicted are evil: but he that is of a merry heart hath a continual feast.''*

When you are happy, your life is a feast whether you eat or not. You won't have an idle mind; you won't be preoccupied with the refrigerator. But your soul is full of God's Word, and you are happy. Life itself becomes your feast. Often depression starts some desire to overeat, and it is good for you not to eat when you are depressed. Instead read God's Word and bring His joy on the scene. It is a bad time to eat when you are emotionally down.

But Nehemiah 8:10 encourages you to *''eat the fat,*

drink the sweet. Go your way, share your portions with others, for the joy of the Lord is your stength."

You will receive far more strength from joyfully eating a small meal than you will from eating a huge feast in sadness. Why? Because God says, "My joy is your strength."

When you bring the strength of His joy into eating your meals, suddenly you get more out of it because your attitude will affect your digestion. Proverbs 15:17 keeps carrying the theme:

> *"Better is a dinner of herbs where love is, than a stalled ox and hatred therewith"* *(Proverbs 15:17).*

Contention and anger make it very difficult for you to digest your food. God says, "Don't eat if you are upset. Get your mind and emotions in control, and then eat."

Proverbs 17:1 says, *"Better is a dry morsel, and quietness therewith, than an house full of sacrifices with strife."*

Going to eat? Then get the strife settled first. If you don't, your physical body is under a lot of self-induced pressure. How do you suppose people get ulcers? How do you suppose people pick up nervous stomach problems such as colitis? Their stomach is already in a knot, and they increase the strain by putting food in there, rather than going to God. Food was never meant to fill up the space; only God can fill it.

Now the Bible goes on and says, *"Hast thou found honey? eat so much as is sufficient for thee, lest thou be filled therewith, and vomit it"* *(Proverbs 25:16).*

Don't be a glutton; don't stuff yourself just because

your favorite food is on the table. Eat what your body can handle, and then stop yourself. God wants us to keep ourselves in line, because if we won't, then we get sick. He created your body; He knows what is the best for it.

Do you want God to give you what is the very best for your body? Then you will love this Scripture. I have used it both in spiritual and natural applications and found that it works both ways:

> *"Remove far from me vanity and lies: give me neither poverty nor riches; feed me with food convenient for me" (Proverbs 30:8).*

You're saying, "God, give me what I need. Get my appetite in line with Your balance for my body, and help me keep it in line."

Sometimes I pray that prayer for spiritual needs, and God will use it in fascinating and wonderful ways. Sometimes I need conviction, sometimes training, sometimes encouragement; but whatever the need it is a way of saying, "When I read Your Word give me what I need."

In the same way, this text can be exactly what you need to acknowledge God's control and get your eating habits in line with His Word. It says:"God—you're the boss, not I. You know what is best, and I trust you for it."

Some people have no problem with temperance in their eating; in fact, they go a step further by abstaining from meats altogether. According to God's Word there is nothing wrong with refusing to eat meat, but on the other hand there is also nothing wrong with eating it.

Whatever you choose is acceptable to God as long as there is thanksgiving:

> *"Forbidding to marry, and commanding to abstain from meats, which God hath created to be received with thanksgiving of them which believe and know the truth. For every creature of God is good and nothing to be refused, if it be received with thanksgiving: For it is sanctified by the word of God and prayer"* (I Timothy 4:3-5).

Whatever you choose to eat, don't forget to thank God for providing it. Before you eat, thank Him; this accompanies the principle of doing all things unto the glory of God, and having a right mental attitude before you eat. Then whatever food you eat becomes set apart, or **sanctified.**

Sanctification of your food through thanksgiving, however, is not simply a way to justify poor eating habits. It doesn't give you an excuse for neglecting proper meal planning. But I believe that if you are ever in a situation where you cannot eat correctly then God can sanctify your food and use it to provide you with proper nutrition.

For instance, in the Old Testament God had a law which commanded the people to allow the soil to "rest" every seven years. During the seventh year the people would not plant anything, and that time would ensure that the soil was its best for supplying nutrients in the food that was grown. Today the soil where we grow food is proven to be depleted of many elements which supply nutrients to food. But I believe you can ask God to bless your meals, and He will provide you with anything that is lacking.

I found a principle in Communion which can be brought into our daily meals. In Acts 27, Paul and several unsaved men went out to sea on a ship, and while they were there they encountered a great storm. It appeared that they would all die, but Paul called the people to fast and pray with him. Even though they were unsaved, they all agreed to fast. Finally, the Word of the Lord came to Paul, and he knew that God would save them. At that time, Paul allowed the men to break their fast:

> "...Paul besought them all to take meat, saying, This day is the fourteenth day that ye have tarried and continued fasting, having taken nothing. Wherefore I pray you to take some meat; for this is for your health: for there shall not an hair fall from the head of any of you" (Acts 27:33,34).

God is so practical; He knows when you need to eat in order to maintain bodily strength and health. Now the men ate meat as Paul had advised them, but Paul ate something different:

> "And when he had thus spoken he took bread, and gave thanks to God in the presence of them all: and when he had broken it, he began to eat. Then were they all of good cheer, and they also took some meat" (Acts 27:35,36).

Why did Paul eat bread instead of meat? If meat was good for their health, why didn't Paul eat meat also? I wondered, "What is happening here?", and then I began seeing a key to his actions. When the Christians in the early church met for communion, they were celebrating the death and resurrection of Christ. In this communion, they ate leavened bread as opposed to the customary unleavened bread in the Old Testament. The only two Old Testament feasts which allowed leavened bread were the feast of Pentecost and the Thanksgiving offering. The only other leavened bread referred to in the Old Testament was the manna which fed the Israelites during their sojourn in the wilderness. Manna was actually "raised bread."

But in the New Testament when Jesus said, "Take, eat, this is my body broken for you,..." He gave the disciples leavened bread, or "raised bread," as it is defined in the Greek.

In 1 Corinthians 11 when Paul reveals God's Word on Communion, he also speaks of raised bread. Why? Because it symbolized the resurrection power of Jesus Christ. In Christ's Body was resurrection life, and Paul was eating this bread in expectancy: he was expecting resurrection power for a miracle after a very difficult experience and fourteen days of fasting and intercession. Because he was drained of strength, he was acknowledging his need for Christ's strength and life. Never take communion expecting anything less.

Now bring the same principle into your daily meals. When you eat, what do you expect from your food? Strength? Food poisoning? When you eat with expectancy of good things from God, you can receive every benefit of its nutrition and maximum strength from it. Whether you eat meat or choose to eat a vegetarian diet, give thanks and eat expecting good things.

Either is all right, as long as you eat unto the glory of God. Don't condemn others for what they eat, but choose what is sufficient and healthful for your own life. Notice that I said "healthful." Romans 14:23 gives an underlying principle for eating right food:

"And he that doubteth is damned if he eat, because he eateth not of faith. For whatsoever is not of faith is sin" (Romans 14:23).

You really know what is right and wrong to eat. You know what is sufficient, and this is saying, "If you're in doubt, then don't do it." If you walk around saying, "I know that I eat too much," or "I eat too many sweets," is that faith? The Bible says that is not faith but sin.

God wants to make you secure and grounded in His Word for your eating habits. Listen to His Word and bring it into your daily meals. Ask the Holy Spirit to guide you in temperance and self-control.

Most of all, remember that we aren't here to pick at each other. God wants to deal with your personal food habits. If someone is overweight don't point at them and say, "He's a glutton."

We aren't here to nit-pick, but we are here to help. Have you ever prayed for that person? I happen to know that there are some skinny people who eat like gluttons, but only they know it. Even if you are naturally slender, God still wants to maintain priority over your eating habits. One man I know is rail-thin, and he told me, "The Lord dealt with me about what a glutton I am, even though I'm so skinny. He told me, 'Get your eating habits in line with My Word.'"

That man repented and began letting the Lord guide him. Today he is enjoying the best health he has ever known. Why? Because when you do **all** according to the glory of God, you bring His perfect balance into your life to enjoy the benefits He promises in His Word. He knows what is best for you; ask Him, and listen to what He says. Enjoy the promise of divine health!

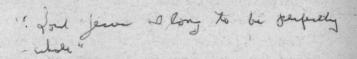

"Lord Jesus I long to be perfectly whole"

Chapter 8

FREEDOM FROM FIASCO

Do bad things happen in groups of threes? Perhaps not, but we all know the feeling of endless traumas when it seems impossible to focus on the "light at the end of the tunnel." These troubles come from many sources, both spiritual and natural. But the important thing is to learn how to shake off disaster and see that there are more for you than could ever be against you!

Have you ever heard the worldly saying that "bad things happen in threes"? (Sometimes it seems as though they happen in tens!) You know the feeling: everything is going along fine, smooth sailing, when suddenly every possible thing in your life goes haywire. I have found that God already knows we're going to run into times of trouble, and that He has prepared us a plan of action for those times. He knows that troubles will come, and He wants to help us in dealing with them without going crazy.

Who brings trouble, or what causes it? John 10:10 says that one instigator of trouble is Satan:

"The thief cometh not, but for to steal, and to kill, and to destroy: I am come that they might have life, and that they might have more abundantly" (John 10:10).

Some people think that God gives them troubled times so that He can make them more faithful; but this is saying that it is not God who brings them, but Satan. How else do crises come? Is Satan the only one who can bring them? 2 Timothy 2:9 says, *". . . Wherein I suffer trouble, as an evildoer."* He is saying, "I sowed trouble and I reaped evil," in other words you can get yourself in trouble; it isn't always the devil behind it.

Some people want to say, "It's all the devil," but don't overlook the fact that you can bring it on yourself by going against God's Word.

Finally, 2 Thessalonians 2:2 identifies another type of trouble:

". . . That ye be not soon shaken in mind, or be troubled, neither by spirit, nor by word, nor by

letter. . . " (2 Thessalonians 2:2).

Your words can be a source of trouble, and God has told us that "out of the abundance of the heart, the mouth speaketh."

If you're always speaking a bad report, watch out. You are looking at circumstances and letting them destroy the power of God's Word in your life. But the fact still remains, every person is going to face times when life seems like one big fiasco:

"Yet man is born unto trouble, as the sparks fly upward" (Job 5:7).

Trouble is no respector of persons. But what about those certain times that just seem to breed troubles? One thing piles upon another, and it seems that things could not be worse even if you had planned them to go wrong.

I remember such a time when Pat Boone came to teach at our church several years ago; it was a miserable situation! For example, the man who introduced Pat took forty minutes in his introduction, and people started getting angry and walking out; the sound system broke down; at a luncheon we held, the waitresses' purses were robbed; and a man also ran in and robbed the money from one of our book tables. Then as one of our staff chased him to recover it, he fell and broke his glasses. My husband became ill, and we had a bad report about our son—every possible thing that could go wrong, went wrong, and people actually wrote hate notes to my ministry.

I know what you think when times like these come: "What did I do to deserve this?" From looking at the situation from the outside you would have thought that we'd done absolutely no planning at all!

I remember the day after all of this happened, I came into my office that morning and was greeted by a very negative financial report. Then with that formality taken care of, my secretary reminded me, "You're scheduled to speak today at a luncheon."

I asked her, "Can't you cancel it?"

Of course there was no chance of cancelling at the last moment, so I asked her to call someone who would go along and pray with me for strength. I gave her a list of people to call, and none of them were available. Then something went wrong with our car, so I had to drive the church van out to this strangely located church across town. I called them beforehand so that I could leave in plenty of time, and they told me, "Be here at 11:00."

"Eleven o'clock? It's a luncheon; I shouldn't be scheduled there until at least noon."

The woman insisted that I be there at eleven, but then when I arrived, the people who were there said, "Why did you come so early? You didn't have to be here until one o'clock."

By this time I just wanted to kick the cat, the dog— anything! So I went into a classroom and prayed, and really repented of my wrong attitude. I said, "Lord, how can I minister to those people, I'm so out of it?" But His answer was beautiful, "You may be out of it, but I'm in it."

At the scheduled time I began to minister, and during the teaching there was a loud popping, cracking noise. A woman jumped up and shouted, "I can move my neck!''

As it turned out, she had been lined up for surgery the next day because two bones in her neck were fused together, and she couldn't move it at all. But God healed her during the teaching, and she was saved and Spirit filled that day!

You need to know that even though troubles come, Jesus comes along with you, and He isn't a respecter of persons either! I saw wonderful results come out of the Pat Boone rally that had appeared to be such a disaster, for one of the women who was saved there brought her family in and then two other families. It all started with something that looked like a total disaster.

I am not exalting trouble, though. When trouble comes you need to be very aware that the devil wants to use it to bring harm your way. Jeremiah 31:20 says, *"...Therefore my bowels are troubled..."* and that refers to your innermost emotions. Often when crises times arise you can get emotional and make wrong decisions out of it.

In Luke 10:41, you see that difficulties can get the best of your temper; you snap at anyone who crosses your path. In this case Martha had come to Jesus in a huff because Mary had left her short-handed of help. Jesus' reply to her was, *"Martha, Martha, you are careful and troubled about many things."*

Troubles fray your temper, and I've never yet known a person who hasn't been guilty of it. But you can also get physically sick from it: *"For my days are consumed like smoke, my bones are burned as an hearth. My heart is smitten and withered like grass; so that I forget to eat my bread. . . . my bones cleave to my skin" (Psalm 102:3-5).*

When times of trouble strike, you lose sleep, you lose your temper, you lose your appetite, you lose your health. It seems that no one is a winner during these times. But it is encouraging to know that God has given us a way out, because when the devil comes with trouble, who comes with us? Jesus.

What about if you suffer because you brought trouble upon yourself? What if you are reaping what you sowed, does Jesus still come? Yes He does.

Jesus still wants to show you where you blew it so that He can deliver you. He isn't concerned about "who is at fault." He is concerned that you get help—His help.

My first advice to you during difficult times is found in Proverbs 25:19, *"Confidence in an unfaithful man in time of trouble is like a broken tooth, and a foot out of joint."* Don't put confidence in an unfaithful man.

Did you ever depend on someone during a disaster and have that person totally let you down? What happened? You put your confidence in a person. The Lord may lead people your way to help, but initially your confidence should be in the Lord. His name is Faithful and True; He'll never let you down.

I found this out and proved it beautifully in my life shortly after the Pat Boone rally. After the rally we found that we were $19,000 in debt. That may not strike you as being a large amount, but that's a lot of money in any economy, and it was even more then. We were to feature a born-again astronaut as a speaker at our church on December 2nd, but then he called to say, "I can't come because of a scheduling conflict. They should never have scheduled me, because it is impossible."

We wondered about scheduling another person to speak, but my secretary said, "Marilyn, I have a very strong inner witness about December 2nd. Don't worry about this speaker's cancellation, because God is bringing us a miracle."

Two days later I was talking to a dear friend, Frances Hunter, on the phone. We were discussing the financial circumstances, and I asked her to pray with me. She prayed, and then she said, "Wait, I have to talk to Charles."

A moment later she returned to the phone and said, "Marilyn, the Lord spoke to Charles and me, telling us to hold a miracle service for you. He said that all of the offering was to go to you also. I believe that God will totally meet your need in that single service—but the only day we're available to speak is on December 2nd."

They came and we held a meeting with 4,500 present. After every expense had been paid, the remainder totalled $19,000. I know from experience that when you hold on, and keep your confidence in the Lord, He will bring faithful friends your way. I thought, "God, don't ever let me be an unfaithful friend, or a foot out of joint."

But you'll find that when you are let down by an unfaithful friend, it is because your confidence was in the wrong place. You should never be confident in anything of a material nature, either. Don't ever put your confidence in money, because the Bible says money can "take wings and fly away." Confidence anywhere other than in the Lord becomes an idol to you.

In the prophet Jeremiah's day, people carried idols around, thinking that they would ward off trouble, discovering the hard way that those idols could do nothing for them. Do you realize that you have to carry idols—but that our heavenly Father wants to carry us? Don't carry an idol, but instead jump up in His arms and He'll carry you through:

> *"And call upon me in the day of trouble: and I will deliver you, and thou shall glorify me"* *(Psalm 50:15).*

Sometimes people will say, "I haven't lived for God, and now I'm really in hot water. I've been backslidden, and you're saying 'Call on Him' now? I think that's hypocritical, I can't do that."

Don't you let the devil sell you that lie! If you are backslidden and you got in trouble, you'd better call on the Lord. Remember, Jesus wants to stand with you against trouble. The Bible says to "Call on Him." It doesn't say, "Call on Him if you've been really sweet, going to church, and reading your Bible."

After you call on the Lord, listen to Him and obey Him. If you're trying to serve two masters, forget it. If you say, "I'm in trouble! Jesus, help me!" but you say and do everything just the opposite, you're trying to serve two masters. After calling on the Lord, remember to let Him be the Lord of your life, and then He'll deliver you from trouble:

> *"Let not your heart be troubled: ye believe in God, believe also in me" (John 14:1).*

When trouble strikes don't let your heart be shaken up. Can you control your heart's response to crises?

157

Jesus said that you can. He wants to shelter your heart against trouble, and He can only do that if your faith is centered on Him. He was saying, "If you're looking at Me, your heart will not be troubled." He gave you a special provision against that fear:

> *"Peace I leave with you, my peace I give unto you: not as the world giveth, give I unto you. Let not your heart be troubled, neither let it be afraid" (John 14:27).*

When you are in the midst of what appears to be a disaster, that's the time to take Jesus' peace. It is a gift that surpasses your understanding; and since it is a gift, all you have to do is receive it. Jesus is called the Prince of Peace. Instead of taking trouble, take His peace. Pray out loud and say, "Jesus, I don't have peace, so I'll take Yours."

Understanding Jesus' peace, it is easy to understand how Paul could make his startling statement, *"We are troubled on every side, but not distressed; we are perplexed, but not in despair;..."* (2 Corinthians 4:8). How could Paul say that? Because He believed Jesus' Word: "Don't let your heart be troubled. Take My peace."

The book of 2 Chronicles describes the wonderful king Hezekiah in chapter 32, not leaving out the many trials that he faced. The Bible is so down to earth that it portrays men such as Hezekiah so that they can be our examples. I saw that the first negative thing in his life began all the way back with his birth: it was his wicked father, Ahaz. He was a terrible man who led the whole nation of Israel into idolatry, and you would imagine that Hezekiah would have been just as wicked as his father. He could have said, "The reason I have so many problems is because I had a terrible father. I'll be terrible because he was terrible."

But Hezekiah didn't look for a scapegoat. You see, Jesus was sent to be our "scapegoat" and bear our blame upon Himself; but before you receive His sacrifice you must first admit, "I'm guilty. I'm a sinner who needs Your righteousness." That's how you get it: by being confident in His forgiveness—not by trying to blame it on someone else.

Hezekiah knew that putting the blame somewhere else would not save his nation. He knew that he needed God—and it's obvious that he needed God's help when you consider the crises of his day!

For instance, natural conditions weren't exactly conducive to peace. There had been a devastating earthquake during Hezekiah's lifetime, in addition to a solar eclipse and a ravaging pestilence of locusts. Then there were the national and political disasters on top of it all. If you think that you have troubles, you haven't seen Hezekiah!

Assyria on the north of Judah was the world power of the day. Egypt was directly on Judah's south, and was the second world power. Consequently, Judah became the "launching pad" for battles between the two countries in their constant wars.

To Judah's west was Philistia, a yet unconquered nation which was constantly muscling in to attack the nation of Judah. Then there was Edom, located eastward, and they also attacked Judah occasionally. There were various hostile governments in Arabia (descendents of the Ishmaelites) who would attack her, and Moab and Ammon, two more nearby countries, were also preparing to wage war. You talk about being troubled on every side, Hezekiah knew what it was about. He had come to the throne in a very serious, politically sensitive time, and he was surrounded with enemies.

But 2 Chronicles tells us that Hezekiah took exactly the steps which we should take against troublesome times in our lives. I love to see how Old Testament examples present such fine figures of New Testament doctrine. Just seeing people act on God's Word can be such an encouragement to us; I know that as you see how God worked during Hezekiah's life, you'll be inspired to know He'll do the same for you.

Here was Hezekiah, sandwiched in the middle of total disaster, with the Assyrian nation coming down to seize his nation. Sennacherib, the Assyrian king, led all of his armies down to Judah, and there they camped, waiting for the small nation to surrender.

> *"And when Hezekiah saw that Sennacherib was come, and that he was purposed to fight against Jerusalem, He took counsel with his princes and his mighty men to stop the waters of the fountains which were without the city: and they did help him"* (2 Chronicles 32:2,3).

Hezekiah reasoned, "If I cut off their water supply, they are going to weaken; they'll have to go home."

What is he doing? In the midst of a very frightful situation, Hezekiah is preparing to win. His confidence is not in men; it is in God, and when you're confident in Him it is easy to make preparation to win, isn't it? Look at all that he did to fortify against the Assyrians:

160

"So there was gathered much people together, who stopped all the fountains, and the brook that ran through the midst of the land, saying, Why should the kings of Assyria come, and find much water? Also he strengthened himself, and built up all the wall that was broken, and raised it up to the towers, and another wall without, and repaired Millo in the city of David, and made darts and shields in abundance. And he set captains of war over the people, and gathered them together to him in the street of the gate of the city, and spake comfortably to them. . . ." (2 Chronicles 32:4-6).

This is very important: when you are in trouble, watch your mouth! Martha complained and Jesus rebuked her. But Hezekiah didn't complain; he went to his people and spoke words of comfort:

"Be strong and courageous, be not afraid nor dismayed for the king of Assyria, nor for all the multitude that is with him: for there be more with us than with him:. . ." (2 Chronicles 32:7).

No matter what kind of fear tries to sieze your heart, you can find assurance in knowing that there are more on your side than there are against you. If God be for you, who can be against you?

Romans 8:31 says, *"What shall we say to these things?. . ."*

What things? The things that are coming against you. You are to speak directly to crises and say, "God is for me, so you cannot be against me." Those are words that bring peace into your life, just as Hezekiah's words brought comfort to his people:

"With him is an arm of flesh; but with us is the Lord our God to help us,..." (2 Chronicles 32:8a).

The king of Assyria could only depend on an arm of flesh: they had no God to help them. What's an arm of flesh? That's an unfaithful friend. That's a broken truth, or a foot out of joint. Don't look at the flesh because it's an unfaithful, unstable place to put your confidence. But Hezekiah said, "God is on our side. We cannot lose," and look at his confession:

"...the Lord our God to help us, and to fight our battles" (2 Chronicles 32:8b).

God is with you against troubles, and He wants you to depend on Him to win the battle. All you have to do is believe and stand on His Word:

"And the people rested themselves upon the words of Hezekiah king of Judah" (2 Chronicles 32:8b).

That's a faith rest, isn't it? How do you keep your heart from being troubled when destruction is all around? You rest in faith on the Word of God: *"Ye believe in God; believe also in me,"* Jesus said. He is the Prince of Peace Who gives you peace to surpass your understanding.

If you will get into your Bible more than ever during times of difficulties, read it, quote it, and take in as much as possible, then you'll have rest. You may say, "They haven't won the battle yet," but they were prepared to win because they were resting in God's Word. The peace that passes understanding is more than enough to hold your faith steady until you get the promise. But you've got to make up your mind to hold on, because the devil wants to steal that peace:

"Thus saith Sennacherib king of Assyria, Whereon do ye trust, that ye abide in the siege of Jerusalem? Doth not Hezekiah persuade you to give over yourselves to die by famine and by thirst, saying, The Lord our God shall deliver us out of the hand of the king of Assyria?" (2 Chronicles 32:10,11).

If ever the devil talked, that was his voice loud and clear. He's saying, "We'll get you anyway. Make it easy on yourselves and surrender." Then they said, "What?" Hezekiah said, "God would save you?"

The devil wants to make you wonder whether God will really deliver you. He'll say, "Don't believe those faith teachers, they're just singing a song. That's idealistic."

That's not idealism—that's realism, because God's Word is The Truth; anything else is a lie. Don't you let the devil cheat you out of your miracle, because he's always been a liar.

"Hath not the same Hezekiah taken away his high places and his altars, and commanded Judah and Jerusalem, saying, Ye shall worship before one altar, and burn incense upon it? Know ye not what I and my fathers have done unto all the people of other lands? were the gods of the nations of those lands any ways able to deliver their lands out of mine hand? (2 Chronicles 32:12,13).

If you'll notice, none of these tricks that the devil used are new ones. He tries them today: "What makes you think you're special?"

Then he'll bring up some broken marriage, some rebellious child, some financial disaster, someone who didn't get healed, and say, "It didn't work for them. Why should it work for you?"

The devil tries to bring up failure to make you cast away your confidence; but God doesn't show you failure. He shows you examples of how you're going to make it. Even the negative examples are to show you how to avoid making other people's mistakes.

Sennacherib just kept hammering away, trying to chip away the faith of the Israelites; but finally the situation turned around:

"And for this cause Hezekiah the king, and the prophet Isaiah the son of Amoz, prayed and cried to heaven" (2 Chronicles 32:20).

They didn't give up, did they? They said, "We're going to win, we're going to win, we're going to win," and they prepared for victory. They stood against the devil. And they prayed.

Then I noticed that the chapter previous to their prayer describes Hezekiah as "God's servant."

I thought, "Oh, God, let me be a servant." Because when you're a servant it's easy to be confident and say, "I'm going to win. I'm going to win." When you make Jesus the Lord over your life, and you are His servant, then you have also made Him the Lord over your circumstances, haven't you? Remember, in order to move in the authority of the Word, you must first be **living**

under its authority. You can only serve one master, and God is the only Master Who can bring you through victoriously.

When you start crying out and interceding to God as His servant, something has to happen. Hezekiah had been speaking God's Word, and the people were "resting" in God's Word, and all of that faith brought angelic activity on the scene. Psalm 103:20 says that angels move at the command of God's Word. Some situations seem so impossible, but maybe you need to bring angels into action! Remember, there are more for you than are against you.

Do you need angels? They won't be active if you're crying the blues instead of speaking faith words. They only move at the command of God's **Word**. I think that some guardian angels are really bored with the people they get stuck with. They think, "How did I get stuck with this assignment?"

Why? Because some Christians are so busy murmuring, moaning and groaning that they won't take time to discover what God says about their situation. But the Word has given us responsibility: "Be strong and courageous, be not afraid or dismayed, for there be more with us than with them!"

"Oh, you mean I have to do something?"

A lot of people expect God to do it all; they gripe and complain and suffer because they think God gave them all of their problems. But God says, "If your confidence is in Me, I'll carry you through your problems."

Hezekiah said, "God will fight our battle!"

What happened? The angels started to move because

God's Word had gone forth. And in verse 21 we can see that only **one angel** got the whole job done:

"And the Lord sent an angel, which cut off all the mighty men of valour, and the leaders and captains in the camp of the king of Assyria. So he returned with shame of face to his own land. . . ." (2 Chronicles 32:21).

Not only did God put Sennacherib to shame, but after his defeat he returned to his own land, knelt down, confused, before his idol, and was slain by his own sons:

". . . And when he was come into the house of his god, they that came forth of his own bowels slew him there with a sword" (2 Chronicles 32:21b).

This is so sad, because here you see how Satan has blinded those people who don't serve God. You see, they may be victorious for a short time. But Satan just uses them, and when he's finished, he destroys them.

Sennacherib's confidence was in himself; his confidence was in the strength of his armies; his confidence was in his idols and his possessions. But your confidence must be in the Lordship of God. Because Hezekiah trusted God, one angel came on the scene and killed 185,000 men: there are more **with** you than are against you.

Will God fight for you? Can He send angels to help you? Yes, He will, if you will look to Him during those times when crises seem to stack up against you.

The Assyrian historical accounts record Hezekiah's victory against Sennacherib, and they say that a plague wiped out the Assyrian army. I thought, "That's even a bigger miracle!" Why? Because this enormous plague hit the Assyrians—but missed the Israelites. That is really a discriminating plague, isn't it? That's the hand of God all the way.

Why such a horrible plague upon so many men? Because they spoke against the living God. No one carried Sennacherib, because he had no living God.

Do you know that this account is recorded in three separate places in the Bible? Not many incidents are written three times, and I asked the Lord, "Why is this in three places?"

He said, "Because I want My people to know what a mighty and loving Deliverer I am during troubled times."

During those times when disaster seems to be lining up against you in every aspect of your life, take heart; have confidence; call on the Lord and obey Him. And remember, there are more for you than there are against you. God wants to carry you through and prove Himself to be **your** mighty Deliverer.

Chapter 9

FREEDOM FROM DEPRESSION

Ruts, slumps, etc.....they're all characteristic of the deadly device of the enemy called
"depression." Is anyone really immune from
it? Although depression is a very real enemy to
faith, you can strip it away in the same way that
Asaph did, as described in the revealing Psalm
77. Look into this man's heart, and you may
find yourself looking into your own.

I just hate depression because it is one of the enemy's biggest lies. He uses it to hold your attention on yourself and your circumstances to keep you from receiving strength from God. I see a lot of believers who are shrouded with depression, and they don't realize that their defeated attitude is just as offensive to God as outward sin. God doesn't want you going through life under a dark cloud; He wants you to rise above it and overcome the situations that keep you depressed.

I found that Psalm 77 unlocks the answer to any depression in your life, for it shows how a spiritual man of God sank into depression, and then rose out of it into victory. The same principle that made him an overcomer in his life can do the same for you today.

Psalming was a beautiful practice that was originated by Samuel when he started the prophets' school. Because many of the students were illiterate, they were instructed in singing God's Word and they would remember it. Have you ever noticed that you remember large passages of Scripture if they are in a song? Psalming was based on the idea that what you might not remember through memorization, you will remember through singing; it worked then, and it still works today. In fact, we are instructed in the New Testament to sing God's Word:

Speaking to yourselves in psalms and hymns and spiritual songs, singing and making melody in your heart to the Lord;..." (Ephesians 5:19).

"Let the word of Christ dwell in you richly in all wisdom; teaching and admonishing one another

*in psalms and hymns and spiritual songs, singing
with grace in your hearts to the Lord"
(Colossians 3:16).*

Psalming is a wonderful way to engraft God's
message into your heart. As a young shepherd boy
David learned to love singing God's Word, and he
practiced it all of his life. He loved to worship more
than any person I have ever heard of; and because he
loved worship, his people were also inspired to worship.
You can imagine how all of this praise started a great
revival in Israel.

After becoming Israel's king, David made
arrangements to have the Ark of the Covenant
transported into Jerusalem and placed on Mount
Zion—practically in his back yard. He was full of the
Spirit, rejoicing in praise on the day the Ark arrived, so
he arrayed himself in a priestly garment and danced and
sang before the Ark, worshiping God with his whole
heart. He was so thrilled with the idea of worship that
he appointed a whole family to worship before it day
and night. The father, Asaph, and his sons would sing
psalms in shifts, and the whole nation rang with God's
praises.

I thought, "What if we held 24-hour praise services
every day?"

What a victorious Church we would be! Praise is the
element which keeps our eyes off of ourselves and on
God and His promises. It causes God's glory to well up
inside your spirit and spill into every area of your life.
Some of the most devoted worshipers I know are also
the greatest soulwinners because people cannot resist
their radiance and joy.

But it amazed me that even Asaph, the great worshiper appointed by David, could succumb to depression. You would think that with all God's praises surrounding him every day he would never fall for that trap; but he fell for the devil's bait, as is described in the 77th Psalm. His account is one that every believer could learn from. I believe that Asaph became vulnerable to depression because he was not devoting enough of his time to God's Word. You might think that because he sang the Word each day he did not need to meditate on it, but I have found that worship in the Spirit will never replace personal study of God's Word. By the same token, God's Word will never replace worship in the Spirit. You need both in your life or you lack balance.

From watching people who work in the ministry I know that many of them think, "I'm around the Word all day, so I can skip my morning devotions."

If ever you need to devote yourself to God's Word, it is when you are in the ministry. You need that strength against the devil's attacks—and they are much more frequent than anything in a worldly job. The same thing applies to people who go to Bible school. Being taught by someone else is not enough; you need to feed yourself.

I have seen people backslide while they were working in the ministry or attending Bible school because they neglect their Word intake. They aren't prepared for the enemy's attacks. God's Word doesn't come in by osmosis, and I think that Asaph may have found that out the hard way.

I know that he has not occupied with God's Word because of the tone he sets in the beginning of the psalm:

> *"I cried unto God with my voice, even unto God with my voice; and he gave ear unto me" (Psalm 77:1).*

This sounds very spiritual and wonderful, but it really isn't. In the Hebrew language he is "crying out in extreme agony," or in today's terms we would say that Asaph is having a big pity party.

A tiny ray of light in the text is his acknowledgement that God heard him. But to be truthful most Christians believe that God hears them or they would not bother to pray; that doesn't mean he is stepping out in a great measure of faith.

So Asaph said, "God heard me," and it seems as though the minute he had God's attention, his confession just went downhill.

> *"In the day of my trouble I sought the Lord: my sore ran in the night, and ceased not: my soul refused to be comforted" (Psalm 77:2).*

If your Word intake isn't high when trouble comes, then a mouse-sized problem appears to be an elephant. A tiny peep sounds like a shriek from heaven. Unless you're looking at the Truth, you become vulnerable to lies. I don't know what Asaph's problems were, but they were probably mouse-sized. The reason I think they were is because I know from experience that every difficulty can seem so much greater at night. Have you ever wakened and started considering your problems? "Oh, God, my situation is impossible!"

I know that Asaph was feeling hopeless because of something he lacked because he said, "My sore ran in the night.'' That sounds terrible, but it doesn't mean that at all. The Hebrew word for ''sore'' is **yad,** and it means ''hand.'' Asaph is really saying, ''I extended my hand to God all night for help.''

Now another bad attitude comes in. While he's holding out his hand to God for help, he says, ''My soul refused to be comforted.''

When some Christians need God the most, instead of running to Him, they run from Him. Asaph is not only depressed, he is getting rebellious. No matter what he knew about God—and he knew a lot—he says, ''I just can't believe that God would help me.''

I know how easy it is to want pity instead of help. Sometimes problems in my life look like mountains, and when I approach someone about it they'll ask, ''How much have you been reading your Bible?''

That isn't what I want to hear. Of course my flesh would much prefer them to say, ''Oh, Marilyn, you poor thing. You work so hard.''

That type of a response won't snap me out of depression, and it never helped anyone. Asaph's crying and griping isn't going to change anything. When he said, ''My soul refused comfort,'' he is really saying that he rejected God's **strength** to be victorious over his depression.

When you run into a major crisis you might ask yourself a question: ''Do I want pity? Or do I want a Bible answer to straighten this out?''

Some of us hit a problem and we immediately rebel. We're mad at God, we're mad at our family, we're mad at ourselves and at anyone else who comes our way.

Even if someone comes to help, our whole attitude is so black that we reject anything they have to offer.

"I remembered God, and was troubled: I complained, and my spirit was overwhelmed" *(Psalm 77:3).*

In saying, "I remembered God," Asaph is remembering God's characteristics as a Judge, not a Father. This is not the way to remember God when you are depressed, unless you just want to be wedged even further away from Him. Sometimes it is so easy to beat ourselves with the Scriptures. Instead of repenting we say, "These just prove I am a failure. God must hate me."

I promise that you'll find plenty of condemning Scriptures to accompany your bad attitude; and you could probably even find some Christians who will be glad to help you. Asaph was remembering God in this way: "He's a big Judge up there with a hammer, out to get me."

Instead of receiving strength, he has gone from depression, to rebellion, and now he is in condemnation. Then he said, "When I complained, it overwhelmed me."

This man is not getting any better; in fact he's getting worse! Look at the way he is praying: he is **complaining**.

Have you ever complained to God? If you have, you probably already know that it doesn't accomplish anything. I've never known God to be moved by complaining. Griping really turns me off, and I have a feeling that it affects Him the same way.

The connotation of the word complain means

"continuous complaining." Here is a picture of Asaph getting on a whining tangent, and it's only digging him deeper into his ditch of depression. When you gripe, your soulish nature overwhelms and buries the work of the Spirit in your life. Of course you're depressed because you're so busy talking that you couldn't hear God if He shouted at you. It would be great medicine to have someone around to say, "Shut up! Just shut up."

Obviously Asaph had no one around to say that to him:

"Thou holdest mine eyes waking: I am so troubled that I cannot speak" (Psalm 77:4).

"God, you're giving me insomnia." That is ridiculous! When we are depressed we can make the silliest accusations. The only positive part of this statement is that he says, *"I cannot speak."*

It sounds as though he has done more than enough speaking, so maybe that's good.

The next verse got me excited, though. In it, Asaph says, *"I call to remembrance my song in the night:..."*

I thought, "He's getting a psalm! Here's the turnaround."

But in the Hebrew he is still not looking to God, he is looking back at some good times in his past. He is trying to take an escape route from his troubles, and from God. I see people do that all the time. They'll say, "I remember when I took a plane trip to Philadelphia and saw the Liberty Bell."

"I'll never forget the first time I saw 'Gone With the Wind.'"

Don't waste your time on escape maneuvers because

they don't work. Have you ever tried to escape by taking your mind off of the problem? You turn on the Late Show, for instance, and they're showing some horror movie. Running from depression is not the answer to the problem because it comes right along with you. God wants to turn depression around, but He cannot help us if we won't let Him.

"...I commune with mine own heart: and my spirit made diligent search" (Psalm 77:6).

What happens when you seek solace outside of God's Word? You don't find it, because you are communing with your own heart, not with His heart. Trying to relive your past is not the answer. Only God's Word changes situations, and it's going to take more than just one verse.

Some people crack their Bibles, read three verses and say, "I read my Bible!" Or they have a very regular Bible reading plan: one chapter a week. That isn't going to cut it. You need to have the ammunition before the battle comes. The tougher your situation gets, the more Word you need to put in. Depression can immobilize you, as it did Asaph, in crisis times. Check your Word level and you will know exactly where you are.

I remember talking with a young woman from Fresno who told me, "I was in the occult, but now I am a born-again, Spirit-filled believer. But in the mornings I have a problem with demonic activity. Voices speak to me when I awaken and I don't know what to do about it."

I asked her how much she read her Bible and she said, "Oh, I read it."

Finally she admitted that she read a few chapters each

week. I then asked, "Do you think you're going to deal with this type of demon problem with only a few chapters a week?"

"What are you suggesting?"

She didn't like the suggestion, either: "Read ten chapters of your Bible every day, get the cassette New Testament and play it from the moment you wake up. Every place you can, listen to it. Fill every area of your life with God's Word."

That girl had a choice: she could have demon activity in her life, or she could have Word activity. The Word is a cleansing agent. The washing of the water of the Word will purge the dirt out of your life; and a lot of Christians go through life with long-term problems because they won't take the trouble to go after them with the sword of the Spirit.

Asaph's whole problem is that he was occupied with himself. When he said, "I communed with my own heart," I wondered what the word "commune" meant. I discovered that its meaning is the same as "complain." Then his spirit made diligent search for something else to gripe about. Once you start complaining you can really develop a good list. Once you start on it, honey, that lists gets really long! Here is Asaph in the depths of depression, and it's his own fault. But he starts blaming God for it.

> *"Will the Lord cast off for ever? and will he be favourable no more? Is his mercy clean gone for ever? doth his promise fail for evermore?"* (Psalms 77:7,8).

He's still looking at God as a judge, and he can't see

any mercy to change his situation. I have heard so many people say, "Will God's Word work for me?"

Not with that attitude it won't. That is rebellion because you shove the responsibility off of yourself and over to God: "God has forgotten me." Asaph is forgetting all of the Word that he knew because of his self pity.

> *"Hath God forgotten to be gracious? hath he in anger shut up his tender mercies? Selah" (Psalm 77:9).*

The word "selah" means "pause and think about that." Here is where Asaph makes his turnaround. He asks, "Has God forgotten me?" He stops and considers the possibility, and of course the answer to his question is, "No." Then he said, "This is my infirmity," and he is realizing that all of his griping is only making him sick. He is remembering his former position in God. Revelation 2:5 tells us that remembrance is a key to change:

> *"Remember therefore from whence thou art fallen, and repent, and do the first works;..."*

Remember what it was to be on fire for God, and then act in the same way you acted then: consume God's Word, and let it consume you. Be in church services, and stay in prayer. When Asaph began looking at the goodness of God he refocused his attention on the Word, and he began to speak it:

> *"I will remember the works of the Lord: surely I will remember thy wonders of old" (Psalm 77:11).*

What were the wonders of old? They were, "God's

deeds that I did not deserve." He was saying, "There was grace then, and there is grace for me today."

You are walking in grace. If you're trying to get something from God on the basis of what you deserve, forget it. But if you remember that His mercy endureth forever, His miracles in your life will come because it's just character to give them to you. He likes to bring you out of defeat because He is wild over you.

Now instead of complaining on all the problems and on how tragic life is, Asaph says, "I'm just going to meditate on Your works in my life, God."

That is meditating on the Word, and the Bible says, *"As a man thinketh, so he is."*

Where is your head most of the time? What do you think about? Is your mind filled with the Word of God? It won't be, unless it's important enough for you to make an effort at it. But when Asaph changed his thinking, then his meditation turned into speaking God's Word because your mouth will speak out of the abundance of your heart. He's not remembering his own ways, he is remembering only God's ways:

"Thy way, O God, is in the sanctuary: who is so great a God as our God?" (Psalm 77:13).

I though I had studied every name of God, but when I looked up this name it was new to me. It is **Ha El,** and it means "the God Who made a plan for you billions of years ago and is bringing it to pass."

Did you know God had a plan for you before you were born? Did you know He had a plan for you billions of years ago? And if He made such a plan, is He going to let you down? No, your problems aren't going to wipe you out. You cannot have a defeated attitude when you know God as Ha El. Suddenly solutions are in sight because He has a plan. Suddenly revelation knowledge flows in because your eyes are off yourself and on Him. To me, the most beautiful part of this passage is that when Asaph looked to God he not only was lifted from defeat, but he even prophesied.

". . . who is so great a God as our God? Thou art the God that doest wonders: thou has declared thy strength among the people. Thou hast with thine arm redeemed thy people, the sons of Jacob and Joseph" (Psalm 77:13b-15).

"You delivered us then; You will deliver us today. Deliverance was in Your plan then, and it is in your plan now."

Ha El has always had a plan for your deliverance. Asaph saw that plan because He started looking at the Word of God. And then he received a vision of the True Deliverer, Jesus Christ, the **Arm** of God. Old and New Testament Scriptures describe Jesus as that Arm:

"Who hath believed our report? and to whom is the arm of the Lord revealed?" (Isaiah 53:1).

"And he saw that there was no man, and wondered that there was no intercessor: therefore his arm brought salvation unto him;. . ." (Isaiah 59:16).

"That the saying of Esaias the prophet might be fulfilled, which he spake, Lord who hath believed our report? and to whom hath the arm of the Lord been revealed?" (John 12:38).

"And I looked, and there was none to help; and I

wondered that there was none to uphold: therefore mine own arm brought salvation unto me; and my fury, it upheld me" (Isaiah 63:5).

God looked upon this earth and said, "There is no intercessor between these people and Myself. But I have planned to send Jesus, the Lamb slain before the foundation of the world."

He brought us salvation with His Own Arm, our Intercessor, Jesus Christ; and Asaph saw the promise of salvation because he began to look at the Word! From the depths of depression he began speaking the Word and identifying with the right Arm of God. Here he describes how God brought the children of Israel out of Egyptian bondage:

"Thou hast with thine arm redeemed thy people, the sons of Jacob and Joseph. Selah" (Psalm 77:15).

Exodus 15 describes God's deliverance of the Israelites, after the miracle of the parting of the Red Sea. Here is the song which Moses sang:

"I will sing unto the Lord, for he hath triumphed gloriously: the horse and his rider hath he thrown into the sea. The Lord is my strength and song, and he is become my salvation: he is my God, and I will prepare him an habitation;... and I will exalt him. The Lord is a man of war: the Lord is his name. Pharoah's chariots and his host hath he cast into the sea: his chosen captains also are drowned in the Red Sea. The depths have covered them: they sank into the bottom as a stone. Thy right hand, O Lord, is become glorious in power: thy right hand, O Lord, hath

dashed in pieces the enemy" (Exodus 15:1-6).

Jesus was at the Red Sea, delivering the Israelites from bondage. He was with Asaph in the night delivering him from depression. And he is with you—and in you—right now to become glorious in power in your life. Now Exodus 15:11 again reveals the arm of the Lord:

"Who is like unto thee, O Lord, among the gods? who is like thee, glorious in holiness, fearful in praises, doing wonders?"

This is the exact part of the Scripture that Asaph was referring to, the Scripture which inspired him to say, "Who is like unto thee, O Lord, among the gods?" Exodus 15 speaks of God "doing wonders," and Asaph says, "I will remember thy wonders of old." It is God's Word that brings deliverance! Then you look into God's Word, and you see Jesus:

"Thou stretchedst out thy right hand, the earth swallowed them. Thou in thy mercy hast led forth the people which thou hast redeemed: thou hast guided them in thy strength unto thy holy habitation...Fear and dread shall fall upon them; by the greatness of thine arm they shall be as still as a stone; till thy people pass over, O Lord, till the people pass over, which thou hast purchased" (Exodus 15:12-13,16).

Asaph says, "Selah," which means, "Pause and consider that." He is saying, "If God did all these things in the past is He going to stop now?"

No! His right Arm has always been ready to provide salvation. Asaph said, "Enemies cannot stand in the presence of your right Arm.''

"The waters saw thee, O God, the waters saw thee; they were afraid: the depths also were troubled" (Psalm 77:16).

This means ''the water saw your signal.''

Moses was standing by the Red Sea, and the enemy army was close behind. There seemed to be no place to escape, as hills and vast wilderness surrounded the Israelies. The Israelites began crying and murmuring just as Asaph had been: ''Oh, Moses, you brought us here to die.''

And literally they were saying, ''You forced us to come here.''

Then Moses said, ''Shut up!'' and he looked for God's answer. God said, ''Raise your arm,'' and when Moses raised his arm the waters of the Red Sea were watching. When Moses raised his arm, at the same time Jesus raised His arm, and the waters had to obey, so they moved back and stood as a wall. Do you want to see your depressing areas back off and stand up so that you can pass through? Then you need to bring the right Arm of God on the scene. God says, ''Troubles, enough is enough. You stand back now.''

When Asaph said that the depths were troubled, he was saying that the water's depths began swirling around. When those Egyptians started through the Red Sea on the Israelites' heels, the waters didn't give them a chance. They fell upon the people with a whirlpool action which pulled them intantly to the bottom. The Egyptians sank as stones.

The last two verses are parenthetical, which means they

explain how the miracle could happen. They describe a picture.

"The clouds poured out water: the skies sent out a sound: thine arrows also went abroad. The voice of thy thunder was in the heaven: the lightnings trembled and shook. Thy way is in the sea, and thy path in the great waters, and thy footsteps are not known" (Psalm 77:17-19).

When I read this in my study I asked, "God, what clouds are you talking about? The Bible never says that it was cloudy and rainy when the Israelites passed through. It says the ground was dry."

Then I found out that this does not signify rain and clouds at all! It is typology for the two people who led the Israelites to deliverance: Moses and Aaron who are referenced in the psalm's last verse. They are the clouds. The New Testament talks about people who will act as though they are clouds; but they have no spiritual knowledge:

". . . clouds they are without water, carried about of winds; trees whose fruit withereth, without fruit, twice dead, plucked up by the roots;. . ." (Jude 12).

God is saying, "There will be people who will make a lot of noise, but they are empty, and they are not people of faith. They are carried about by every wind of doctrine, and it destroys them."

It makes me think of the saying of "The emptier the can, the louder it rattles." These clouds are full of noise, but they accomplish nothing. 2 Peter 2:17 mentions them again:

"These are wells without water, clouds that are carried with a tempest: to whom the mist of darkness is reserved for ever."

Who are these clouds? They are people who have not based their lives on the rock of God's Word.

But Asaph is talking about the clouds as people who thundered out the voice of God; and that God's Word shot forth as arrows. He turned his attitude around and received revelation knowledge of what went on in the spiritual realm when God delivered His people. And God showed him, "I can do it for you, Asaph."

It is so beautiful that Asaph said, "Thy way is in the sea, and thy path in the great waters, and thy footsteps are not known" in Psalm 77:19. What path is he talking about? He is talking about the path of grace. God asked me, "Did the Israelites deserve the miracles they received?"

"No. They were murmuring."

"But they got them anyway."

They were walking in the footsteps of grace. And Asaph is saying, "I'm going to walk in those footsteps too."

They walked in the Word of grace; you walk in the Word of grace. Maybe they didn't deserve it, but they got the miracles anyway. If Asaph got what he deserved, he could not have had God's strength. If we got what we deserved, God would have nothing to do with us. But it's grace that you have to walk in.

You say, " I thought it was by faith, not by grace."

Yes, but you receive grace through faith. Oh, maybe you have been complaining and murmuring just as the

Israelites, and just as Asaph were. But there are footsteps of grace for you to walk in when you repent of your depression. When you are really depressed your first step should be to crack your Bible and start reading. Then take another step and say, "I'll remember God's grace toward me." Take a third step by meditating on it and making it yours.

What will happen? You'll be following the same footsteps of grace which Asaph walked in. He said, "First I meditated, then I talked."

When you start meditating and then speaking God's Word, then you start walking God's Word. You start walking in light, guided by His right Arm, Jesus. Walk with Him in the footsteps of grace and you'll be full of rain and thunder, shooting forth fiery arrows of God's Word. The waters of depression in your life have to stand back when you let Ha El be the Planner, and you let Him deliver you with His Arm.

Chapter 10

FREEDOM IN A RIGHT SELF IMAGE

Sometimes it seems that many of us fall short of our calling because we aren't even sure what it is! Even if we are sure of exactly what God has for us, a lot of us are "out of focus," and not fulfilling. God has a special way for us to get out of wrong self images by adjusting our focus and getting back "in sync."

God has an image of you as an individual. He's not just racking up numbers like a big computer, but He is keenly aware of every person as an individual who is uniquely created to His praise and glory. It is so important that you understand what His image is of you, and that you shed any false images in your life now. Sometimes it's easy to take on a negative self image because we compare ourselves with others, and God has warned us about the dangers inherent in such comparisons:

"For we dare not make ourselves of the number, or compare ourselves with some that commend themselves: but they measuring themselves by themselves, and comparing themselves among themselves, are not wise" (2 Corinthians 10:12).

It is easy to measure ourselves against others and then think, "I'm such a failure; I fall so short." But the world's image is not the one God wants us to look at. Genesis 1:26 tells us that God made us in His image: *"Let us make man in our image, after our likeness. . . "* God made us in His Own image which He planned for us before we were made. We were to be like Him. We lost that likeness when Adam sinned, but we have now gained it back in Jesus. Now Romans 8:29 reveals even more about our image:

"For whom he did foreknow, he also did predestinate to be conformed to the image of his Son, . . . " (Romans 8:29).

God is saying, "I knew you so intimately that I even knew the decision you would make. And when you made that decision, you had a special plan and image: to look just like My Son."

God has a way for you to reveal His Son as nobody else can. But if you were to ask most Christians, they could not tell you exactly how to step into the fullness of that image; they don't know what God has for them personally. I think that one of the reasons for their misunderstanding is because they are often trying to be like somebody else. How often do we try to emulate someone whom we admire or respect? I think that all of us have done it.

If you try to take on characteristics of someone that you admire, you get out of your own image—that may not be God's image for you. There have been times when I have felt strong respect for people and wanted to be the way they are. For instance when we were young in the ministry I was very moved by the outstanding prayer ministry of a woman in our church. In our daily prayer meetings she was never through praying at the hour's end. She wanted to continue in prayer for five or six more hours, and sometimes she would. I so admired her diligent prayer and thought she was so spiritual, that I decided to take on a similar ministry. I asked her, "Did you know that God has called me to be an intercessor just as you are?"

When she said, "No, Marilyn, I didn't know that," it really let the wind out of my sails. But I'm glad that she answered in such a way because that was not the image which God had for me. I wanted to slip into that image because I thought so highly of her, but God showed me, "Don't wear someone else's image; I have one that fits you perfectly."

But most of us wonder, "How do you find it?"

I have found that it isn't as difficult as it may seem. I

know that God wants to make it easy for you, not difficult. One man says, "Make it hard on God and easy on yourself." I believe the Lord doesn't want to make it hard on you to fulfill your image. He wants you to roll your faith over on Him and let Him reveal His plan for you. Your job is to believe what His Word says about your image:

"But we all, with open face beholding as in a glass the glory of the Lord, are changed into the same image from glory to glory, even as by the Spirit of the Lord" (2 Corinthians 3:18).

You take on your image by holding the face of the Lord in Whose image you were created. Behold the face of the Lord by looking to Him. Sometimes we get our attention distracted from our true image because we behold other people's faces or circumstances. We had understanding of who God wants us to be in His kingdom, but because we don't keep beholding Him, we lose our image instead of growing more glorious in it. God wants us to be diligent in keeping our true image so that we go from glory to glory in it, improving all the time as we look more like His Son.

Perhaps you have an image of yourself as a tremendous soulwinner. You won't be fulfilled and happy serving the Lord until you are moving forward and growing in that image. If your call is to be a tremendous Sunday school teacher—and be assured that God has called you to be more than "good," He wants you to be the best—you will only recognize fulfillment in your image by beholding His face and being changed into His image. By beholding Him your image becomes glorious.

Of course the devil wants to pull you off your course, away from God's true image for you. He doesn't want you going from glory to glory because it shatters his kindgom. He wants to stagnate Christians in their walk by stagnating them in their image. I believe that many Christians today are discontent simply because they don't know how to walk in God's image for them. Many are frustrated because they once tasted of their image, but they slipped out of it by not beholding their Father's face. They instead beheld the faces of other people or the cares of the world. What happened? Their image was choked out of their lives.

I read a story about a man who knew what image God had for him, but he was convinced of his inability to achieve it. When I read it I wondered, "Lord, how many true images are never fulfilled because we fail to realize Your ability in us?"

This story proves to me that when God looks at us, He sees all the potential of Himself within us to accomplish our tasks. If we had to fulfill His image of us through our human ability, we could achieve nothing.

The man in the article I read was a fifty year-old farmer who was well seasoned in his ability to farm, as he'd done it all his life. He was also illiterate, and could not read at all. When the call of God came on his life, he immediately focused in on his illiteracy; he beheld his own inadequacy instead of God's perfect adequacy. The Lord spoke to him saying, "Go and preach My Word."

But the man argued, "God, how can I preach? I cannot even read, so how do You expect me to preach?"

The farmer had an image of himself as an illiterate farmer; but that was not God's image of him. God was seeing him as having His Own potential to fulfill the call, so He kept convincing the farmer in his heart. Finally the man broke down and wept while he was working one day. He cried, "God, I'm too old to go to school. At fifty years old how can I enter the first grade? I feel so defeated."

He began interceding and waiting on the Lord, crying and pouring out his heart. He was beginning to behold the Father's face; and at the end of his intercession, although God did not speak to him again, he felt a peace welling up within his heart.

That evening as his wife read from the Bible, she stumbled over a word and he leaned over and told her, "That's inhabitant."

She read further, but he was still unaware of the change effected from within. She struggled with another word as he skimmed the page and said, "That's impoverished."

Suddenly an awe filled him as he told her, "I never memorized those verses. I'm reading! Give me the Bible."

Praise God, that man began to read as though he'd been reading throughout his life. He had been beholding the Lord, and he moved into his true image. Job 32:8 reveals how God can bring such a transformation:

"But there is a spirit in man: and the inspiration of the Almighty giveth them understanding" (Job 32:8).

Jesus Christ indwelling you by His Spirit will give you

every facet of understanding that is necessary for you to fulfill your image. If you need supernatural power, He will give it to you. Colossians 2:9-10 says that *". . . in him dwelleth all the fulness of the Godhead bodily. And you are complete in Him, . . ."*

If God has an image of you being the best soulwinner in your city, within you is His Spirit with every ability that you need. If your image is one of a vital supportive ministry, or an evangelical outreach, don't you dare look at yourself and say, "I can't do it." Make it hard on God and easy on yourself by acknowledging His ability within you.

By beholding His face you recognize His ability, so if you lack a right self image, you gain freedom in it by letting Him create it in you. If you have slipped out of a right self image you can behold Him and see its restoration. Some of you reading this have been "out of sync" with your image: God has one image of you, but you are bound by a wrong image of yourself. You sense in your heart God's plan for you, but because you have blown it, the devil has lied, "You'll never be a success again. What makes you think you'll go from glory to glory? That's only for winners, and you're a failure."

But the Bible describes the life of a man who had a mighty image, but stopped beholding His Father's face and lost the image he once had. The encouraging part is that he regained his true image in the end, and was more glorious in his latter image than he was in his former; you can discover from his example how God can restore a lost self-image, and even make it better than it was before!

Just as He saw you and made a plan for you, God

made a plan for this man long before his birth, and his image was even prophesied back in Genesis 49 when Jacob prophesied to his sons before his death. Jacob (whose name God changed to "Israel") was the father of twelve sons, each of whom founded Israel's twelve tribes. In Jacob's prophesy he spoke of a tremendous image when he prophesied over his son, Dan:

> "Dan shall judge his people, as one of the tribes of Israel" (Genesis 49:16).

He is saying, "A judge over the tribe of Israel will come from the tribe of Dan." It is very easy to take this prophesy for granted; it is one of those Scriptures where I never really looked further to see why the Bible is giving that information, yet it is a very significant Scripture. I can remember reading the book of Judges and finding that most of Israel's judges originated from the tribe of Ephraim, not from Dan. As I studied it I found that only one judge came from the tribe of Dan, and that man was Samson.

God had an image of Samson before his birth; and He had an image for you before your birth. Samson's image was further enhanced when an angel appeared to his mother to foretell his conception:

> "...Behold now, thou art barren, and bearest not: but thou shalt conceive, and bear a son" (Judges 13:3).

Then the angel said, "This is no ordinary son, for he is the one who will begin to deliver you Israelites from the hand of the Philistines."

Samson's name meant "sun-like," and God set him apart before his birth to shine as a light and deliver his people. The prophecy must have been a breath of fresh air for the Israelites' desperate souls because the Philistines were cruel taskmasters. No doubt the prophecy was "sun-like" in these dark times of oppression. The Philistines were from the Mediterranean coast, and they were a very strong and aggressive race of people. Slowly they infiltrated the Israelite tribes until the day came when none of the Israelites were even allowed to have knives or weapons in their possession. Philistine governments soon established their authority in such force that even work tools were monitored. Samson's life was greatly heralded because Israel was anxiously awaiting such a deliverer. The angel did not say that he would totally deliver Israel from their grip, but that he would begin the task. His leadership was also foreknown because of the prophecy in Genesis 49. He had a mighty image.

The angel told Samson's mother-to-be, "This child's image is so important that he is to be separated to God from birth by a Nazarite vow. His image is so important that even before his conception you will separate him to God by observing that vow in your own life until his birth."

What marvelous preparation for the image of a deliverer. Samson was born to fulfill it, and he was prepared through a Nazarite vow. In this vow which ordinarily lasted sixty to ninety days, a person was not allowed to eat or touch any unclean thing, or drink of fruit of the vine. Our equivalent of this vow today would be a time set apart unto God for prayer and fasting. You say, "It's legalistic to make vows."

I have found that these types of vows are highly

honored by God. They are a specific time where we behold His face. He can really use them to help bring us into our true image. I know that God used the vow to keep Samson's eyes on Himself, and on the special call to be a deliverer from the Philistines. And from Samson's youth the Spirit of God enabled him with all the ability to fulfill and carry out that image.

The inspiration of the Almighty within you will give you any supernatural element you need to fulfill **your** image, too. Remember, make it hard on God and easy on yourself.

The Spirit of the Lord began moving Samson into feats of supernatural strength early in his life when he lived in the camp of Dan between Zorah and Eshtaol. Now if God was planning to use Samson as Israel's deliverer, He would have to endow the man with the ability to deliver. Judges 14 describes the might and strength which God put within Samson for his task:

> *"And the Spirit of the Lord came mightily upon him, and he rent him as he would have rent a kid, and he had nothing in his hand: but he told not his father or his mother what he had done"* (Judges 14:6).

When Samson was traveling with his parents, he came across the path of a young lion, and the animal began to growl and roar against him. To protect his life, the Spirit of God endowed him with the ability to rip that lion to pieces as though it was a young pup! I think that even Samson himself was surprised at his strength. Later on, when the Philistines came against his plans to marry one of their women, Samson was aware of his strength and he reacted brutally:

"And the Spirit of the Lord came upon him, and he went down to Ashkelon, and slew thirty men of them, and took their spoil, and gave change of garments unto them which expounded the riddle. And his anger was kindled, and he went up to his father's house" (Judges 14:19).

Where did Samson get his strength? He was given strength from the same One Who created him for the purpose of delivering the people. He had strength from the Father as long as he beheld his face. I think that Samson had a very spiritual background as he was an Israelite judge. He knew what his calling was, and he knew that God had physically equipped him for it.

When Samson's own people started feeling the pressure back from the Philistines after Samson began to fulfill his calling, they said, "We'll get rid of this troublemaker once and for all; he's really causing problems with the Philistines. If we deliver him to them, then they'll see how peaceful we are, and they'll leave us alone."

They bound Samson with cords, but the Spirit of God came upon him to keep Israel's deliverer from beging destroyed:

". . . the Spirit of the Lord came mightily upon him, and the cords that were upon his arms became as flax that was burnt with fire, and his bands loosed from off his hands" (Judges 15:14).

That's the power of a deliverer who knows God will give him what he needs to live out his image. Whatever God has called you to do, just keep beholding His face and He will make you more glorious in it each day. If

He called you to be a missionary just keep beholding His face; He knows how to make you the best missionary you could be; and you'll look just like Him.

If you are beholding His face, you will be the best in whatever God has called you to do. You won't be comparing yourself with others. You won't be bringing confusion or division. You will be building up the Body of Christ. Because God is an Edifier, you will edify others also.

While Samson kept his eyes on the Lord he was growing into his image of a deliverer. But Judges 16:1 tells us that Samson took his eyes off of what God had for him and got out of sync with God's image:

"Then went Samson to Gaza, and saw there an harlot...."

He took his eyes off his true image and began beholding a harlot. Now his image began to change as he became involved with adultery. God wanted Samson to deliver people from the Philistines—not get involved with their women! Now he was beholding the face of the enemy.

I see people come to the Lord and experience instant deliverance from their old nature. They are full of the joy of the forgiveness and reconciliation with Him that comes to those who are first saved, delivered, and Spiritfilled. You see them begin to mature and blossom in their walk with the Lord, but then they stop beholding His image: their true image. Often the Holy Spirit will alert me to pray for them because suddenly they are no longer growing. He says, "They are out of kilter with God's image."

One night my husband awakened with a start and named a certain person, saying, "He is drinking again."

How did he know that? It was because the Holy Spirit gave an alarm to stimulate intercession on that person's behalf. People slip into their former state when they aren't beholding their image and being transformed into it from glory to glory. Faith never stagnates: either it moves backward or forward. When you aren't moving forward from glory to glory it is probably because you need to behold His image.

Samson's vision was no longer centered on his calling, but it was on the pleasures which he found in the enemy's territory. He ended up with Delilah, and here is the tragedy of the story: not only did he lose his vision—he lost his sight. Now he couldn't see natural things to get an image. The Philistines offered Delilah the equivalent of $4,000.00 to betray the source of Samson's strength. That is a lot of money in any economy, and it turned her into a deceiver. She learned that his strength would vanish if his hair were cut off, and when he fell asleep with his head in her lap, she had the scissors ready. Samson was delivered to his enemies weak and powerless. The Bible says, "He became as other men."

When you take your eyes off of your image you become as other men, too. The devil wants you to think, "People will accept me if I'm not so different. I have to compromise somewhere."

That is a lie. When you turn from your true image in Jesus Christ you are bound by the world's image and you become just as everyone else. That's when people say, "If that's a Christian I don't want to be one."

Your true image in Christ makes you special. Don't let the world strip it away from you; don't take your eyes off God's image of you.

I love the way God handles His people. He doesn't say, "You big backslider!" and slam you against the wall. He doesn't say, "You big sinner, why did I pick you anyway? You were nothing but a mistake."

No, God does all that He can to place you back into His image for you. Samson's eyes were blinded and he was given women's labor, grinding at the mill stone. But although his natural eyes were sightless, something else began bringing his image back into focus: his hair began to grow long again. I can picture Samson touching his hair and getting a picture of his true image in his heart. He began to say, "I'm still a deliverer. I'm still a judge and a deliverer, no matter where the enemy puts me."

He had his chance to prove it shortly afterward when the Philistines gathered to worship and honor a pagan idol, Dagon. They assembled together and, being bored, called for Samson to ridicule: "Some deliverer!"

When Samson was brought forth he renewed his image, and in the few short verses describing his renewal you will find the key to your image in Christ. Whether you need image renewal or you need to understand the perfect likeness of Christ in you, the secret is found in the four meanings of the word "renewal."

The first meaning is "To change into clean garments." What is this cleansing? It is repentance. When you repent of whatever you have had your eyes on (whether intentional or not), then you are receiving the robe of Christ's righteousness, the clean garment he shed his blood for you to have.

"And Samson called unto the Lord, and said, O Lord God, remember me, I pray thee, and strengthen me, I pray thee, only this once, O God, that I may be at once avenged of the Philistines for my two eyes" (Judges 16:28).

The words for "Lord," and "Lord God" are key words explaining how you can be restored into God's true image for your life. When Samson said, "LORD," (as it is shown in the King James text), he was acknowledging God as **Jehovah,** the Revealing One. He is saying, "You have revealed my image to me."

But then the text reads "Lord God," and these are two more names for God. The word God means "Elohim," the God of power and strength. Samson knew God as might and strength; he was well-acquainted with supernatural power for being Israel's deliverer. But what he hadn't known before now was that God was also his "Lord," which is the word "Adonai." It means "Master," or "Owner."

We can say, "I have my image! God gives me the strength and power to fulfill it." But if you aren't allowing Him to be the Master of your life and letting Him call the shots, you can get out of image. God wants to be your Master and Owner, as well as your Savior. That is where Samson had missed it. Now he was praying, "God, You be in charge; You let me fulfill the image that You called me to in the first place." This is Samson's prayer of repentance. His change of heart made him a different man: again, he was the deliverer God called him to be!

I hear a lot of people speak very negatively about Samson, and they love to use him for a bad example.

But God showed me a different angle of his life as a deliverer. He showed me that he was the only deliverer of his time. Not one person ever stood with him; in fact they stood against him. Samson stood on God's image for him, and he stood alone.

When you see Christians slip out of their image, don't be too quick to criticize. Were you praying for them? We need to support the Body, and if we prayed, these situations would be a lot less frequent. Samson may have fallen, but in the end he was renewed. After repentance, his second step of renewal was "revival." This aspect means "to make young," and "to strengthen." After he repented, Samson knew that God wanted to **strengthen** him with the strength that was necessary to be his people's deliverer. His image was brought back to life, enlivened with God's supernatural power which would enable him to be strong in his image.

The third aspect of renewal means "to go forward." Here's the forward-moving faith that accompanies an image: you go from glory to glory. Samson mentally returned to the knowledge and awareness of being a deliverer. When you return to the image, that's when you move forward in it.

"And Samson took hold of the two middle pillars upon which the house stood, and on which it was borne up, of the one with his right hand, and of the other with his left. And Samson said, Let me die with the Philistines. And he bowed himself with all his might; and the house fell upon the lords, and upon all the people that were therein...." (Judges 16:29,30a).

Here is the fourth meaning for "renewal;" it is "regeneration." It means "to be placed back in image." This is the active work of the Holy Spirit: *"Not by works of righteousness which we have done, but according to his mercy he saved us, by the washing of regeneration, and renewing of the Holy Ghost" (Titus 3:5).*

The Holy Spirit is the One Who will restore and uphold you in your true image. He is the One Who will reveal that image to you. He placed Samson back in image when he began pushing against those pillars, and the balcony came crushing down. The Bible tells us that Samson *"slew more at his death... than they which he slew in his life" (Judges 16:30b).*

Was he a deliverer? On that day he caused the death of almost all of the prominent Philistine leaders. He completed his image, and was buried between Zorah and Eshtaol, the place where the Spirit of God first moved him in feats of supernatural strength. *"Having begun in the Spirit shall we end in the flesh!"* No! You are going to end in the Spirit just as Samson did. If you need freedom from a wrong image, the Bible has an answer for you. If you need to be freed into a right image, the Word of God tells you how:

"Be not conformed to this world, but be ye transformed by the renewing of your mind...." *(Romans 12:2).*

Transformed in what way? Into the image of Jesus Christ, from glory to glory. Only when your mind is renewed will you "prove what is the good, and perfect, and acceptable will of God." Try to prove that good, and perfect, and acceptable will of God without keeping your mind renewed; you cannot do it. You have to stay in the Word of God and let it immerse you and transform you into His image. When you stay in God's Word, you will be transformed into His image, and that word "transformed" means "transfigured."

When Jesus stood on the mount of Transfiguration he glowed. As your mind becomes renewed to God's Word, you will be transfigured into His radiant likeness. People will be attracted to you because you are full of His light.

Pray this prayer with me: "Dear Father, I praise You for working mightily in me to will, and to do Your good pleasure. Fulfill in me Your image, and let me grow in its glory each day. I thank you Father that I am being transformed as I fulfill my image by beholding You in Your Word. Today I have a new focus of Who You are in me; and I know that you will bring me from glory to glory, strength to strength, and faith to faith. In Jesus' Name, Amen.

Receive Jesus Christ as
Lord and Savior of Your Life

The Bible says, "that if thou shalt confess with thy mouth the Lord Jesus, and shalt believe in thine heart that God hath raised him from the dead, thou shalt be saved. For with the heart man believeth unto righteousness; and with the mouth confession is made unto salvation" (Romans 10:9-10).

To receive Jesus Christ as Lord and Savior of your life, sincerely pray this prayer from your heart:

Dear Jesus,

I believe that You died for me and that You rose again on the third day. I confess to You that I am a sinner and that I need Your love and forgiveness. Come into my life, forgive my sins and give me eternal life. I confess You now as my Lord. Thank You for my salvation!

Signed _____

Date _____

Write to us. We will send you information to help you with your new life in Christ. Marilyn Hickey Ministries • P.O. Box 10606 • Denver, CO 80210

**Let us join our faith with yours
for your prayer needs. Fill out below
and send to:**

Marilyn Hickey Ministries
P.O. Box 10606
Denver, CO 80210

Prayer Request _____

_____

_____

_____

_____

_____

Name ^{Mr. Mrs. Miss}_____

Address _____

State _____ Zip _____

Phone _____

TIME WITH HIM BRINGS MIRACLES

YES:

☐ Please send me your free monthly magazine **Time With Him** (including daily devotionals, timely articles and ministry updates).

☐ Please send me Marilyn's latest tape catalog.

Name _Mr. Mrs. Miss_ _____

Address _____

City _____

State _____ Zip_____

Phone ( ) _____

For information regarding Marilyn Hickey's monthly Bible reading program, you may write:
TIME WITH HIM • P.O. Box 10606 • Denver, CO 80210

TOUCHING YOU WITH THE LOVE OF JESUS!

24-Hour Counseling and Prayer
LIFELINE

When was the last time that you could say, "He touched me, right where I hurt?" No matter how serious the nature of your call, we're here to listen, offer solutions based upon the Word, and show you how to touch Jesus for real answers to real problems.

**Call us anytime day or night,
and let's touch Jesus, together!**

**(303) 777-5029
WE CARE!**

About the Author

Marilyn Hickey, Founder and President of Marilyn Hickey Ministries, is being used by God to "cover the earth with His Word." Her teaching ministry, beginning in the United States, has now developed into a worldwide, outreach via radio, television, books, cassette tapes, personal appearances and seminars.

Marilyn is answering God's call to awaken the "sleeping giant" of Christian laymen by revealing that the authority of God's Word is a creative source, full of life changing power.

Millions of lives, all over the world, have been brought out of defeat into victory through Marilyn's simple, yet dynamic, conveyance of Biblical truths. She has also been responsible for establishing Bible Distribution Centers designed to distribute Bibles to people in foreign countries regardless of their race, creed, or color. Israel, the Middle East and South Africa have been especially receptive.

In addition to her teaching ministry, Marilyn is also a busy wife, mother and homemaker. She is married to Wallace Hickey, the pastor of Happy Church in Denver, Colorado.

Marilyn can best be described as someone "bubbling with enthusiasm while radiating God's wisdom and revelation."

BOOKS BY MARILYN HICKEY
ORDER BLANK

BOOK TITLE	CODE	PRICE EACH	QUAN.	TOTAL PRICE
Beat Tension	I	75¢		
Change Your Life	V	75¢		
Conquering Setbacks	C	75¢		
Divorce Is Not The Answer	D	$2.95		
Egypt Revisited In Prophecy	H	$1.95		
Experience Long Life	Z	75¢		
Fasting & Prayer	W	75¢		
Fear Free, Faith Filled	U	$3.25		
Gift Wrapped Fruit	O	$2.00		
God IN You, TO You, And FOR You	AA	$4.95		
God's Benefit: Healing	P	75¢		
God's Covenant For Your Family	S	$4.95		
God's RX For A Hurting Heart	Q	$3.25		
God's Seven Keys To Make You Rich	N	75¢		
Hold On To Your Dreams	Y	75¢		
How To Become More Than A Conqueror	K	75¢		
How To Win Friends	J	75¢		
I Can Be Born Again	EE	75¢		
I Can Dare To Be An Achiever	FF	75¢		
Keys To Healing Rejection	M	75¢		
Motivational Gifts	X	$3.50		
#1 Key to Success—Meditation, The	BB	$2.50		
Power Of Forgiveness, The	B	75¢		
Receive the Evidence of the Spirit-filled Life	DD	$3.95		
Renew Your Mind	E	75¢		
Signs in the Heavens	GG	$4.95		
Speak The Word	A	75¢		
Standing In The Gap	L	75¢		
Treading With Angels	F	$2.95		
Winning Over Weight	T	75¢		
Women Of The Word	G	75¢		
Your Miracle Source	R	$2.50		

Prices subject to change without notice

TOTAL

Please Print:

Name Miss Mrs. Mr._____

Address _____

City _____ State_____ Zip_____

Phone (_____)_____

Circle One:

____ __ __ __ __
Please print number   Expiration date

_____
Signature

Mail to:
Marilyn Hickey Ministries
P.O. Box 10606
Denver, CO 80210
(303) 698-1155

--Notes--

Pg 13 dont hating yourself

Pg 15 Unequally goked re longone

Pg 31 fear 32

Pg 38 excellent dont see crom on place 6
      defeat

Pg 48 tonght never —

Pg 52
   53 We need to do after God.

Pg 58 govern for my need

Pg 176 depression

Pg 73 dont kith very foul

--Notes--

—Notes—

—Notes—